T0329963

Economic Science and Practice

Economic Science and Practice

The Roles of Academic Economists and Policy-makers

edited by

Peter A.G. van Bergeijk

De Nederlandsche Bank

A. Lans Bovenberg

CPB Netherlands Bureau for Economic Policy Analysis

Eric E.C. van Damme

Center for Economic Research, Tilburg University

Jarig van Sinderen

Netherlands Ministry of Economic Affairs

Edward Elgar
Cheltenham, UK • Lyme, US

Published by
Edward Elgar Publishing Limited
8 Lansdown Place
Cheltenham
Glos GL50 2HU
UK

Edward Elgar Publishing, Inc.
1 Pinnacle Hill Road
Lyme
NH 03768
US

A catalogue record for this book
is available from the British Library

Library of Congress Cataloguing in Publication Data

Economic science and practice : the roles of academic economists and
    policy-makers / edited by Peter A.G. van Bergeijk . . . [et al.].
    Includes bibliographical references and index.
    1. Economic policy. 2. Economics. 3. Economists. 4. Government
economists.   I. Bergeijk, Peter A.G. van, 1959–   .
HB74.P65E356 1997
330—dc21   97–24222
                                                                CIP

ISBN 978 1 85898 690 6

Printed and bound by CPI Group (UK) Ltd, Croydon, CR0 4YY

Contents

PART III ECONOMICS AND SOCIETY

Figures and Tables

Contributors

Peter A.G. van Bergeijk, Monetary and Economic Policy Department, De Nederlandsche Bank.

A. Lans Bovenberg, CPB Netherlands Bureau for Economic Policy Analysis, Research Centre for Government Policy (OCFEB) at Erasmus University and Center for Economic Research (CentER) at Tilburg University.

Harry P. van Dalen, Research Centre for Government Policy (OCFEB) at Erasmus University Rotterdam and Netherlands Interdisciplinary Demographic Institute.

Eric E.C. van Damme, Center for Economic Research (CentER) at Tilburg University.

Reiner Eichenberger, Institute for Empirical Economic Research at Zurich University.

Bruno S. Frey, Institute for Empirical Economic Research at Zurich University.

L. Ad Geelhoed, Netherlands Ministry of Economic Affairs and Erasmus University Rotterdam.

Alexis Jacquemin, Université Catholique de Louvain and European Commission.

Arjo Klamer Erasmus University Rotterdam and George Washington University.

Edmond Malinvaud, College de France.

Richard Portes, Centre for Economic Policy Research and London Business School.

Thomas C. Schelling, University of Maryland, School of Public Affairs.

Jarig van Sinderen, Netherlands Ministry of Economic Affairs and Research Centre for Government Policy (OCFEB) at Erasmus University Rotterdam.

Jules J.M. Theeuwes, Leyden University.

Acknowledgements

One of the unpleasant aspects of being an editor is that you have to make difficult decisions. Given the available space and the extent of the international market we had to make a selection of the many excellent papers that were presented at the conference 'Economic Science: An Art or an Asset' helping to sharpen our perspective on the relationship between economic science and economic policy.

We benefitted a lot from the papers by Hans Borstlap, Cees van Gent, Dick Wolfson and Gerrit Zalm and the comments by Frank den Butter, Patrick van Cayseele, Raymond Gradus, Hans Hafkamp, Hans Opschoor, Hans Vijlbrief and Bert de Vries. Fortunately, the Research Centre for Government Policy (OCFEB) at Erasmus University Rotterdam is simultaneously publishing the Papers and Proceedings of the workshops (van Bergeijk, Bovenberg, van Damme and van Sinderen 1997). Equally important for the success of our venture was the role of the chairmen at the conference: Wim Duisenberg and Ruud Lubbers.

Sander Baljé, Mandy van Gelder, Frank Hindriks, Thomas Grosfeld, Peter Koster and Ben Vollaard provided valuable library services. Harry van Dalen and Gilbert van Hagen helped in the organization of the conference.

1. Introduction: High Tech or Human Capital?

Is a trend visible towards sterile economics? Is the Queen of the Social Sciences becoming a science that can be characterized by the triad 'pure, abstract and essentially aesthetic'? Are we moving towards a new style of economic analysis? The superfluous use of mathematics, the relative importance of theory *vis-à-vis* empiricism, education, and training of economic doctorates have been critically discussed in leading journals such as the *Journal of Economic Literature*, the *Journal of Economic Perspectives* and the *European Economic Review* and in books such as *The Making of an Economist* (Klamer and Colander 1990).

American economics has been contrasted with European economics which is said to be more policy oriented and to pay more attention to institutional and historic aspects of the economy (Portes 1987, Kolm 1988; in 1995 a special issue of *Kyklos* was devoted to this topic). The argument is that European economists play an important role in the policy process, whereas their American colleagues are confined to academia.

A discussion that is cast in terms of American economics versus European economics runs the risk of making a caricature of much of the economic analysis that is taking place on both sides of the Atlantic. Indeed, the utility of geographically determined archetypes or role models is questionable. It is probably more appropriate to discuss the future development of economics in terms of 'high tech' and 'human capital' economics. With 'high tech' economics we mean a sterile, formalistic non-contextual approach. The 'human capital' approach involves high quality applied research that is transparently linked to the 'real world'.

Many economists have expressed concern with the present situation and we are now all quite familiar with discussions about the merits of the two archetypes of economics. Economics is not the home of a happy family: theory and practice are divorced (or at least living apart). Is the breach permanent or can the spouses be reconciled? And why did the breach occur in the first place?

1.1   Academics and Policy Advisers

Central to any analysis of the relationship between policy and science is the exchange of ideas between the academic (the scientist, the tool-maker, the discoverer) and the policy-maker (the decision-maker, the tool-user, the practitioner). On the one hand, this is a symbiotic relationship because well-trained economists and well-founded economic research are important inputs in the process that transforms economic knowledge (together with other scientific achievements and political constraints) into policy. Moreover, academic economists and economists in government fight essentially the same battles against economic twaddle (that is, lay beliefs, opinions and perceptions that ignore scientifically established empirical regularities and relevant theoretical insights). Henderson (1986) attacking 'do-it-yourself economics', van Sinderen (1992) confronting 'pre-economic thinking' and Krugman (1996) castigating 'pop internationalism' are all part of the same mission, namely to drive out prejudice, superstition and metaphysics from the policy debate. Academic economists and policy-makers are thus natural allies to some extent.

However, the symbiosis is far from perfect. There is a wide gap between the focus, emphasis and tone of the academic side of our profession and that in the trenches (Harberger, 1993). Indeed, frictions exist between these different breeds of *homo economicus*. These frictions constitute the *leitmotiv* of this book. It should be clear by now that we will not be concerned with situations in which academic economists reveal faulty reasoning or ideology on the side of the policy-makers or where policy-makers point out the irrelevance (both empirically and politically) of specific theories and theorems. In those cases policy-makers and academics communicate and the market for economic ideas functions well.

In contrast, we are interested in situations where communication is lacking, where academics are disinterested and policy-makers ignorant. In those cases frictions between policy-makers and academic economists develop into barriers to exchange (of ideas, of policy questions, of facts, of visions). Let us consider some factors that may explain these frictions in a bit more detail.

The different roles of economists

Frictions between policy-makers and academics partly originate in confusion about the different roles that economists play in society. Scientists have a different function than the policy-makers and the two roles require different skills. The policy-maker typically cannot make a useful analysis by considering the implications for a narrow field only. To function effectively the policy maker has to efficiently synthesize and integrate existing knowledge. In order to put forward policy advise that is both rational and relevant, one has to be a philosopher, one has to be 'learned'. Relevance, rather than logic, ultimately drives the argument.

The expected benefits of the division of labour are an important incentive to specialize in the economic profession (just as in ordinary life). According to Stigler (1963, pp. 10-11), specialization is the royal road to social and scientific recognition. Indeed, the complexity of economic issues may have encouraged 'high tech economics'. Incidentally, the resulting pattern of specialization does not assess individual or national capabilities. People specialize according to their *comparative* advantage. Hence economists may specialize in a subfield in which they have an absolute disadvantage. Alternatively, an economist may choose not to specialize in a field in which he or she has an absolute advantage. Consequently, some policy-makers are excellent theorists while some academic economists provide excellent policy advice.

Galbraith (1972) offers a more sociological explanation for the lack of communication between practitioners and academics. Building on the sociology of tribal groups, Galbraith argues that there is a natural desire to delineate insiders and outsiders. The prestige system of economics assigns the lowest position to economists that are dealing with practical issues while, according to Galbraith, at higher levels in the pecking order economics divorces itself fully from practical questions and from the field of other scholarship.

This puts [the man who deals with everyday policy] in commmunication with the world at large. As such he is a threat to the sharp delineation which separates the tribal group from the rest of society and thus to the prestige system of the profession. Moreover, his achievements are rated not by his professional peers but by outsiders. This causes difficulty in fitting him into the professional hierarchy and argues strongly for leaving him at the bottom. (Galbraith 1972, pp. 40-42)

Intensive specialization is thus necessary if one wants to be a successful academic economist (but it is obviously not sufficient). An economic practitioner, however, has to be a generalist. Policy problems of modern society are so complex and academic specialization has gone so far that a team of specialists would probably become unmanageably large and at some point a generalist is needed. Who ensures that the team of specialists is well-composed? Who manages the team? Who explains the results to the decision makers (especially if they are not trained in economics)?

The lost art of economics
Somewhere along the tracks we have lost the art of economics out of sight. Colander (1992) uses Keynes's (1891) three-part distinction between positive economics, normative economics and the art of economics to argue that positive economics is not the appropriate methodology for applied economics (that in Keynes's definition comprises policy advise). In addition to the traditional textbook exposition that makes the positive-normative distinction, it is useful to distinguish the art of economics as a separate methodological category:

• a positive science (a body of systematized knowledge concerning what is);
• a normative science (a body of systematized knowledge discussing criteria what ought to be); and
• an art (a system of rules for the attainment of a given end; its object is the formulation of precepts).

According to Keynes, confusion between these three methodological categories is common and the source of many mischievous errors. Colander (1992) argues that the advance of economic science is hindered by the binary positive-normative distinction that characterizes economic methodology since Friedman's (1953) 'Methodology of Positive Economics': 'Positive economics suffers from the lack of an art of economics because, if a separate art is not delineated, positive economic inquiry faces pressures to have policy relevance, which is constraining to imaginative scientific enquiry' (Colander, 1992, p. 194). Also economic policy-making, however, is hindered by this misunderstanding of the proper place of applied economics. Due to uncertainties and the importance of non-economic aspects, applied work, which is policy relevant, often involves a substantial extent of judgement. Consequently, many academics perceive such work as being subjective:

> That's wrong. All economic analysis - positive, normative and art - should be as objective as possible. Good applied economic work tells people how to achieve the goals they want to achieve as effectively as they can. No normative judgments about those goals need be made, and the analysis should remain objective. (Colander 1992, p. 195)

Indeed, the art of application should not be met with academic disdain. Whereas both positive and normative analyses are probably best pursued in academic freedom, an intensive communication between practitioners and academics might provide the most fruitful soil for the art of economics.

Fogging
A lack of communication between academic economists and policy-makers is a matter of bad marketing. The academic discourse is not cast in a language that policy-makers appreciate. The articles in the leading journals (indeed many of the profession's products) are too complex to be absorbed when policy is being formed. Academic books, reports and articles bear little resemblance to the typical work product of a non-academic economist. In order to get published, the academic economist has to conform to the style of the present economic discourse. Arthur explains that a clear writing style was a barrier to publication for his now classic 1989 *Economic Journal* article 'Competing Technologies, Increasing Returns and Lock-in by Historical Events':

> I was at pains to keep the ideas in the forefront and not buried under a lot of theorems and pseudo-mathematical verbiage. I [...] decided to write the paper in an accessible, informative style. Given the current economics editorial process, this proved to be disastrous [...] I put the paper through eight rewrites

[...]; each time it became stiffer, more formal, less informative and possibly as a result more publishable'. (quoted in Gans and Shepard 1994, p. 173)

As a consequence of the implicit style guide of the top journals, many papers in economics can be characterized by the following model:

- facts are stylized facts, not broad uniformities;
- formal structure is emphasized;
- the 'interpretation' of the theory (that is, how it links up with the 'real world') is not provided; and
- predictions are not confronted with the data.

This suggests that theory has become detached from the real world and hence from policy. This distance between policy and science has increased over time. It is not a natural division, because economics was born in the policy debate. In fact, many top economists have been policy-makers. Ricardo (who is often seen as the prototype of the neoclassical economist) actually may have served as a role model for European economists such as de Grauwe or van der Ploeg who presently are Members of the Belgian and Dutch Parliament, respectively.

Mental inertia

Harberger (1993, p. 1) defines the policy economists as 'the ones who struggle in the field to harness the knowledge and insights from economics science to help improve the economic organization of their countries and the economic life of their peoples'. He writes (p. 3) that 'the life of the economic policy practitioner is very demanding, and requires sharp eyes, subtle perceptions and artfully moulded prescriptions'. Helping one's country must be a highly satisfactory activity because most policy-makers, according to Harberger (1993, p. 1) 'have to endure in frustration, waking up every morning to go out and fight battles they rarely expect to win'.

Indeed, as Tinbergen (1952) already pointed out, the execution of rational policies is often impeded by the tendency to maintain the *status quo* and by personal and institutional inertia. An 'aversion of the complex' may influence economic policy wrongly:

Many officials ... dislike to accept somewhat more complicated reasonings or the results of calculations even if from the scientific point of view they are decidedly better than the rules of thumb often accepted before. (Tinbergen 1952, p. 77)

Tinbergen's observations suggest that *new* insights are rather difficult to implement, because policy-makers both need to break new ground and to understand difficult analytical issues in evaluating the proposed policies. Policy-makers, however, do not hold a monopoly on mental inertia. The idea of supply side policies, for example, initially met considerable scepticism not only from economic practitioners but also from academic economists. Indeed, many viewed the idea that the distortionary effects of a tax might matter as pure ideology without a scientific foundation. Such incentive effects are now part and parcel of the economic tool box. Indeed the flows of both new theoretical insights (often developed by academic economists) to policy-makers and empirical insights (often discovered by practitioners) to academics seem to occur at a rather slow pace. This suggests that increased personal mobility between the academic spheres and the policy quarters would help to improve the communication.

The Case of the Netherlands

In their 1993 article on American and European Economics and Economists, Frey and Eichenberger discussed the Netherlands as an example of a European country where the influence of (former) economics professors on policy is substantial:

In December 1991, there were the following professors of economics in the cabinet of the Netherlands alone: Jacob E. Andriessen (University of Amsterdam) as Minister of Economic Affairs, Jo Ritzen (University of Rotterdam) as Minister of Education and Science and Jan P. Pronk (University of Amsterdam) as Minister for Development and Cooperation. Moreover, Wim Duisenberg (University of Amsterdam) was president of the Dutch Central Bank. (Frey and Eichenberger, 1993, p. 187)

In support of Frey and Eichenberger, we add that at the end of the cabinet period de Vries (the minister of Social Affairs and Employment) became professor at the Research Centre for Economic Policy at Erasmus University while Lubbers (Prime Minister) became professor at the Center of Economic Research at Tilburg University.

Andriessen retired and Zalm (a former director of CPB and professor at the Vrije Universiteit) became minister of Finance in the new Cabinet keeping the academic content at a high level (the other professors remained in the Cabinet).[1]

Does this imply that the Netherlands is developing the role model for the European way of bridging the gap between science and policy? Or is the Netherlands simply lagging behind and is the American approach creeping in? The results of van Dalen and Klamer's review of Dutch economists (Chapter 4) suggest the latter: the style of research is becoming more American and less Dutch (see van Winden 1995 for a similar opinion). Also Geelhoed's description of the Dutch situation (Chapter 9) illustrates that economic education and research are rather 'American' than 'Dutch'. Three workshops organized early 1996 by the editors of this volume revealed that a gap exists between theory and policy in the Netherlands even with respect to the very core of economics (for example, policy-makers and academics disagree on the question of whether a better functioning of the market mechanism will improve macroeconomic performance).[2] A recurrent theme was the difficulty of getting the economic recipe accepted by policy-makers (especially if they have no training in economics) and getting academics involved in relevant research. At about the same time, however, leading Dutch economists moved from academia to policy. The typical and unclear Dutch situation may explain why the present volume has grown from a conference held in the city of the Hague, the government centre of The Netherlands.

1.2   Plan of the Book

This book is based on papers presented at the conference 'Economic Science: An Art or an Asset?' which was held in January 1996 in the Hague. The conference was organized by the Research Centre for Economic Policy (OCFEB at Erasmus University) and the Center for Economic Research (CentER at Tilburg University) in close collaboration with the Economic Policy Directorate (AEP) of the Netherlands Ministry of Economic Affairs.

Both the editors and the contributors are a balanced mix of economic practitioners, disbelievers and pure scientists. While the editors are from the Netherlands, the contributors are from both continents, thus offering a balanced perspective on the American and European role models of economic science.

Part I deals with economic role models, thus setting the stage for the book. Two different views on the link between economic science and policy-making are presented. Frey and Eichenberger argue in Chapter 2 that economics departments are increasingly less relevant for the analysis of actual policies and institutions, that economists do not face sufficient incentives to conduct policy-oriented work, and that the globalization and Americanization of economics harms the contribution of economics to the art of policymaking.

Portes (Chapter 3) disagrees on all these three fronts. Modern economics has produced insights that eventually became very relevant to policy-makers, economists are pushed too much to produce applied research that is useful in the short term, and the standards set by the global and US community of economic scientists help to produce the best results in the long-run, also for those interested and involved in policy-making.

Van Dalen and Klamer more closely explore the differences between European and American economists in Chapter 4. They distinguish three different characters: the 'researcher', the 'policy adviser' and the 'academic professional'. Typically, the 'researcher' applies existing knowledge and techniques to real world problems and is willing to compromise but unwilling to sell his product (that is, to put it to the market test). The policy adviser aims to enlighten the policy process with scientific insights. The third archetype, the 'academic professional', is committed to the academic game, which is not set up with the intention to serve society. Their survey of Dutch economists shows a remarkable difference with Klamer's earlier findings during his 'conversations' with US economists. For example, in contrast to their American counterparts, Dutch economic PhD students consider a good working knowledge of the economy, its (recent) history and its institutions important for becoming a 'good' economist.

Theeuwes (Chapter 5) argues that economics is the art of persuading one's audience. Our understanding of a complex world is at best very limited. Hence Truth does not exist. Economics is rhetoric; economics is about making a good case. The successful economist does not strive for a balanced view: he develops one side of the argument by selecting appropriate examples and arguments and by leaving out any evidence that might damage the case. To maximize the benefits of specialization, economists should specialize in particular views. Theeuwes expects policy-makers and politicians to judge which economic advocate has the most convincing case.

Part II provides two case studies of the interaction between policy and economic science. One of these studies takes the European perspective, the other one illustrates the American perspective. Jacquemin explores in Chapter 6 how the modern theory of industrial organization has contributed to European competition policy. In his view, this theory has provided a rich framework for discussing the problems and trade-offs that policy-makers face. However, due to a lack of observations, policy-makers have to make presumptions and shortcuts on the basis of their beliefs when facing these trade-offs.

Schelling (Chapter 7) sees the main role for economists as helping public policy to arrive at rational choices by making transparent the costs and benefits of considered policy actions. Schelling is rather sceptical about the impact of economic thinking on public policy in the US, with the exception of defence policy where game theory made a major contribution.

Part III addresses the roles of applied and theoretical economics in modern society, from the academic and the policy point of view.

In Chapter 8, Malinvaud (while recognizing the limitations of economics) stresses that modern economics has made major contributions to economic policy-making. He argues that academic economists should refrain from taking sides in debates if conclusions are not clearly determined. Given the state of economic science, economists (both in academia and in policy-making) should be eclectic and draw on various theories. Malinvaud stresses the merits of the Tinbergen view that the choice of policy objectives should properly be in the domain of the politicians, but that the results from economic research should not be unduly influenced by policy-makers. The royal road to better economic science and economic policy is more balanced teaching that stresses economic intuition.

Recognizing the importance of academic independent judgement as a major force against ideological policy-making, Geelhoed in Chapter 9 argues that the globalization of economics and the resulting dominance of the US role model are a threat to the quality of policy-making outside the US. Conforming to the standards and requirements of the US market, European academic economists have lost touch with the institutional context of their own countries. This is a pity because they educate new generations of policy-makers that are increasingly trained to solve the problems of the US at the cost of neglecting the macroeconomic problems and specific distortions of the European economy.

In Chapter 10, we argue that diversity in economic analysis is beneficial: it is the logical consequence of the principle of the division of labour. The demand for the services delivered by economists has grown tremendously; economics has developed into an industry and there has been a continuous increase in the degree of specialization of economists. Some economists mainly focus on the building of new specialized tools and models while others mainly devote themselves to providing policy advice. Extensive specialization, however, is possible only to the extent that communication is swift and intensive. Robinson (1933, p. 1) already noted that 'The gap between the tool-makers and the tool-users is a distressingly wide one' and she suggested that 'The practical man must be asked to have patience, and meanwhile the economist must perfect his tools in the hope of being able sooner or later to meet the practical man's requirements'. Meanwhile, the practical economist has waited for 65 years, the market for economic ideas has grown, specialization has increased further, and the gap has widened (possibly due to a longer chain of intermediaries between theorists and practitioners).

We venture to state that the problem is that most academic economists are in close contact neither with experts in other fields nor with the practitioners. Like Duisenberg (1997), we believe that the world will end up a somewhat better place to live in when we succeed in linking the academic profession more closely with the world of the practitioner. It will enrich the discipline of economics and lead to better policy.

Notes

1. It should be noted that the market position of Dutch economists in polity is not as strong as the quote from Frey and Eichenberger suggests. For example, one of our contributors, Ad Geelhoed, secretary-general of the Netherlands Ministry of Economic Affairs and former chairman of the EU's Economic Policy Committee is a lawyer by training.

2. The Research Centre for Economic Policy Research (OCFEB) Rotterdam simultaneously publishes a report on the workshops that were organized as part of the conference and that deal with the case of the Netherlands more specifically (van Bergeijk, Bovenberg, van Damme and van Sinderen 1997).

PART I
ECONOMIC ROLE MODELS

2. Economists: First Semester, High Flyers and UFOs

Bruno S. Frey and Reiner Eichenberger

Economists are fond of calling economics the 'queen of the social sciences'. Though this is not all too kind to the neighbouring social sciences, this claim is not unfounded. There are three major reasons why economics may be considered 'queen':

- Economics is the only social science whose stars are crowned with the Nobel Prize;
- The economic approach is applied and is prominent in the other social sciences;[1] and
- Economics plays a large role in society, especially via economic policy.

However, a sceptic might retort the following. First, the Nobel Prize is not wholly due to economics being superior to any other social science but that it has an effective lobby in the form of the Swedish Central Bank which donated the funds at its centennial (see Lindbeck 1985). The prize for economists thus does not go back to Alfred Nobel.

Second, there are also large areas in the social sciences pursuing quite a different approach (for example, discursive theory, structural theory, or the many variants of systems theory), or worse still, are not even aware of the rational choice approach.

Third, the heydays of Keynesian business cycle policy are long over (and it has been debunked by economists themselves), and the specific proofs of the influence of present day economics on society are scarce. Not even economists are able to come up with much evidence (see Faulhaber and Baumol 1988). There are even scholars who jokingly claim that economists tend to worsen economic conditions, or leave them unaffected. A recent example is Barro's (1993) newspaper essay on the relationship between the chairmen of the Council of Economic Advisors and the state of the economy which states:

> The sad conclusion is that economic outcomes (measured by the contribution to the misery index) and the credentials of the chairman of the council (measured by the citation count) are essentially uncorrelated. Although some who are highly ranked on citations ... do well on performance, the highly ranked Mr. Schultze ends up with the worst economic outcomes. Moreover, some of the chairmen who are ranked low on citations ... emerge with good economic performance.

While Barro's essay is certainly meant to be a joke (not least for methodological reasons which are so obvious that they do not have to be pointed out), it may still indicate that economists' claim of how useful they are is not especially well founded today.

This chapter endeavours to analyse present-day economics by applying the tools of economics: we present an *economics of economics*.[2] Following the rules of our science, we want to *explain* how economists act, and to *predict* how the field is going to look like in the (near) future. Only at the end we add our evaluation which for some of the readers - especially economists - may appear too critical. The reader should, however, bear in mind that the authors are fully convinced that economics has been making excellent contributions to understanding reality and will continue to do so in the future. We are proud of being economists, which is exactly the reason why we also point out developments in economics that we consider to be negative, and even destructive.

We distinguish two quite different types of economics which we label the 'core' and the 'rays' (section 2.1). Based on this distinction, section 2.2 offers four propositions on the state of economics. Counterarguments are extensively discussed in section 2.3. The future development of economics which we consider to be likely is sketched in section 2.4 and we investigate the possibility of endogenous limits in section 2.5. Section 2.6 discusses new possibilities to change the evaluation of economists from PC (Publications and Citations) to a more encompassing PEP (Professional Evaluation Procedure). The last section offers conclusions.

Perhaps the most controversial finding is that economics - in the sense of a science enlightening us on problems in our society - will prosper *outside* economics departments, that is, in law, history, sociology, political science and psychology. The remaining small departments of economics will mainly be staffed by scholars who look at this science as a branch of mathematics: they essentially deal with self-defined problems within formal structures.

2.1   Two Kinds of Economics

It is useful to differentiate two types of economics, labelled the 'core' and the 'rays'.

The Core

The core of economics is 'neoclassics'. Following Becker (1976, p. 5) it is defined by three characteristics:

- Individuals maximize (or at least relentlessly pursue) their own, essentially egoistic, preferences;
- Humans systematically respond to relative prices: a relative price rise *ceteris paribus* reduces the quantity demanded, and increases the quantity supplied; and
- There is a strong tendency towards equilibrium between demand and supply.

While Becker considers all these requirements to be essential, others (for example, Alchian, 1977, Chapter 7) only emphasize the first two. Other typical characteristics of the core of economics may be mentioned - such as the use of a common language - but the three points suffice to clearly differentiate economics from the other social sciences which lack such a common core. We do not claim, of course, that economists are completely homogenous and would all agree to this characterization of the core.[3] Nevertheless it seems to us to be a fair picture.

The demand for the insights produced by the core is external to academic economics. It is sought by the public which wants to have an interpretation of reality from the economic point of view, and specifically by institutions such as the government which wants economic policy advice and private firms which hire people trained in that approach. Students choose economics as their subject because they are aware of this outside demand.

We contend that this core of economics essentially covers what is contained in a simple textbook or what is taught at a good university in the first semester. The professional discourse therefore neglects it as trivial and takes it as a matter of course. To learn the core is not intellectually difficult. But its reasoned application to local, regional, national and international problems which has to take into account the prevailing institutional conditions and facts is demanding. The incentives of economists employed at a university to apply this core are the prestige, as well as the money gained from professional advice as well as a career as politician, top bureaucrat or in the Central Bank (Frey and Eichenberger 1992 and 1993).

The Rays
Academic economic research is composed of a great number of specialized sub-fields which emanate from the core. Such rays are characterized by three major aspects:

* output is self-defined;
* rays are highly specialized; and
* the strong influence of fashions.

Output
The output produced is self-defined by the international economics community and is measured in terms of scientific publications and citations in professional journals. Articles in scientific reviews do not mainly serve to propagate knowledge but act as a selection device for academic economists. Ray-economics is thus inward oriented.[4] The topics and questions dealt with are theory-driven (Mayer 1993), and the task is to (marginally) improve on existing formal models which in turn are based on previous formal models. What matters is technical rigour and formal elegance. The presentation of the results is highly regulated (for example, Holub 1990 and 1992).[5] Content is only relevant as far as it gives a reason to apply a certain technique

of analysis.[6] The same holds for institutional knowledge.[7] Content and institutions are disregarded because they are irrelevant for the self-defined quality standards. The quality of a professional contribution can only be evaluated with respect to internationally valid aspects. Formal rigour and elegance perfectly meet this requirement: the quality of the proof of a theorem can be judged by other scholars irrespective of whether they live in Bonn, Madison or Hongkong. In contrast, academic contributions based on an extensive knowledge of local conditions and institutions cannot be judged by an external scholar. To give an example: if a Dutch economist writes an economic study on Amsterdam's police department, it cannot be evaluated on its merits by a scholar not intimately familiar with the conditions prevailing in Amsterdam. This restricts the range of evaluators to a few academic economists, presumably scholars living in that city or at least in the Netherlands. The impersonal scientific 'objectivity', a major standard in this type of economics, is then at risk because the few evaluators almost certainly know each other well, resulting in judgements biased by non-scientific considerations. If they are friends, the evaluation is too positive, if they are foes, it may be too negative. As a result, scholars who endeavour to participate in the prestigious and career enhancing international market for economists refrain from doing that kind of work as it is not acceptable by the respective community of economists. Only those who do not aspire beyond the local market for economists can afford to work on topics with an emphasis on local data and institutions.

In economics composed of rays, originality and innovation are also muted. Such thinking is acceptable only within the strict limits set by orthodox formal theory, and refers therefore at best to new types of techniques rather than to content. This is a consequence of the now common use of (at least) two independent referees in most good professional journals. It is almost impossible to find two scholars sympathetic to a new idea; at least one of them most likely clings to the well-established orthodoxy. The chances for young economists - from whom one may expect more new ideas - are even slimmer. It has been empirically established (Hamermesh 1994) that unknown contributors tend to get unknown referees while established scholars are provided with well-known referees. The unknown referees are often graduate students and assistant professors in the editor's own university who for career reasons must demonstrate that they are well versed in advanced (ray) economics. They will therefore be reluctant to favour new ideas because these are, almost by necessity, less rigorous and formally elegant than small variations of an accepted model. Thus we agree with Arrow (1995, p. vii) who says:

> I think the publication selection procedure at the major journals has become methodologically more conservative, more given to preferring small wrinkles in existing analyses to genuinely new ideas.

The same bias against novelty holds for research grants. According to Friedman (1994, p. 199), 'Funding [by the National Science Foundation] has stifled innovation. "Peer reviews" favour established scientists and directions of research.'

Specialization

Rays are highly specialized. An extreme form of division of labour is used to raise productivity and output. The rays are still connected to the core as the respective assumptions (for example, utility maximization) are followed but the abstract pursuit of a special topic takes prominence. The links to the core are the weaker the more highly developed a ray is. Connections to other rays rarely exist, and over time rays typically become more, and not less isolated.[8] Indeed, an economist doing research in one ray does not need to know much, if anything, about other rays. Accordingly, cross fertilization is rare.

Fashion

Rays are much influenced by fashions. The development of a particular ray formally resembles the spread of a disease or - to put it more positively - a product innovation.[9] There is one (or a few) economist propagating an idea. If lucky, further economists are early followers. The high point is often marked by an authoritative survey by one of the main proponents. Many economists then join the ray as late followers. Then the ray dies but is sometimes reanimated years later. This development may be illustrated by three examples: growth theory, social choice theory and capital theory.

Growth theory was 'founded' by Harrod's 1939 article, and was later followed by Domar (1946) and the neoclassical version by Solow (1956 and 1957). The culmination of this (now called 'old') theory was marked by Hahn and Mathew's (1964) survey. Provided an article is considered 'significant' (as done, for example, by Holub et al. 1991) if it has been cited at least 30 times, then the last 'significant' article was published already in 1970. But until then, that is from 1939 to 1970, only 52 per cent of all articles on economic growth were published, and almost half (48 per cent) were still to come. The share of followers, and the time in which they prospered, was thus extremely long, that is, economics fashions have a long unproductive life even according to the standards of ray-economics (citations). In the meantime, growth theory has been reanimated but it is noteworthy that it essentially links up to Solow (1956).

Social choice theory dealing with the formal problem of preference aggregation is another fashion. In its modern version, it goes back to Arrow (1951) and the much less noted work by Black (1948). The culmination is Sen's (1970) survey book, but since then there has been a huge stream of articles and books.

Capital theory was created by Robinson, Kaldor, Sraffa and other Cambridge (UK) economists as an attack on the Cambridge (Mass.) neoclassics championed by Samuelson and Solow. The high point of the intensive debate is marked by Harcourt's (1972) and by Blaug's (1975) evaluative surveys. Today this ray is almost forgotten, but at its culmination it was the leading economists' preferred ray.

Obviously, rays may be of unequal intensity, and have unequal success and longevity.

The demand for rays

The demand for rays is almost completely internally driven. It serves as a professional selection process for the academic career (the barriers are the various exams ranging from the diploma, doctorate, *habilitation*, to appointments as assistant professor), to the position of scholars in the prestige hierarchy, and rewards in terms of income and prizes. The standards imposed are designed to maintain self-defined quality, and are signalled by the number, timing and ranking of journal publications.

The American market for academic economists is by far the most developed with respect to standard setting.[10] Its signalling system is such an efficient indicator of who is capable to function well in ray-economics that it is spreading quickly around the world. As these signals can best be learnt in the country of origin, there are practically no economists doing research in a ray who would not have spent an extended period in the United States. 'Many take from the US their professional standards, their views of what are the interesting problems, and their approach to them' as Portes (1987, p. 1330) revealingly writes. Scholars doing research in a ray - for the members of this type of economics this is the *only* kind of acceptable research - can be called *high-flyers*. Their aim is to push a particular ray as far as possible - Krugman (1995, p. 43) even speaks of a *Blitzkrieg* approach. The heights reached are defined according to the professional standards, that is, the extent of rigour and formal elegance, but it bears no relationship to the insights gained into the working of the economy and society. There are even those who completely lose contact with the ground and the core of economics, and who completely live in a self-constructed world of formal problems. We therefore call them *UFOs* (Unidentified Flying Objects) also because to an observer outside ray-economics they appear mysterious.

Relationship between Core and Rays
Figure 2.1 illustrates how the rays are attached to the core of economics. The figure reveals that there are many specializations (rays) at the same time. They originate from the core but some are more broadly, and others only thinly attached, that is, they are more self-reliant and self-referring. They are of different height, that is, in a different phase of development, or have proved incapable to match the rigours and formal elegance of other rays. Finally, the rays are only related through the common core, that is, a typical ray-economist knows next to nothing about another ray, and does so without much damage. Thus, a respected economist is able to write in 1995: '... laboratory experiments which are not possible in the social sciences' (Aoki 1995, p. 31) though 'experimental economics' is one of the most rapidly growing rays. Similarly, most ray-economists are

not even aware that there exists an 'economics of culture' (or they choose not to define it as a serious ray).

Figure 2.1   The core-ray conception of economics

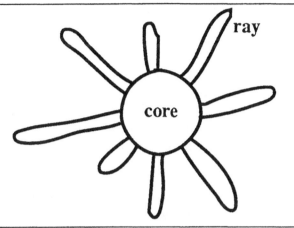

Figure 2.1 may look quite different according to the point of view chosen. Consider Figure 2.2. The left-hand side picture represents the perception of an outside observer. He or she sees the large core and pays little or no attention to the rays.

Figure 2.2   Outside and inside view of economics

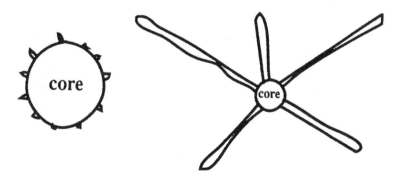

The right-hand side pictures the view of a (well-informed) member of the *'de facto* nomenclatura' (an expression used for ray-economists by Krugman, 1995, p. 33) or of the 'econ tribe' (an expression coined by Leijonhufvud, 1973): in academic research, the core is unimportant, and all that matters are the rays.

2.2   Basic Propositions

On the basis of the characteristics of the core and the rays we advance four propositions:

> *Proposition 1: Rays are the more important within economics, the more intensive international competition among economists is.*

When the research output of economists has to be evaluated across nations, there are few members who are able to evaluate the facts and institutional background. Quality can only be judged by resorting to established, self-defined standards of rigour and formality, and hence the research performed in a ray.[11]

> *Proposition 2: 'Good' economics departments are ray-focused.*

The qualification 'good' refers to the standards reigning in the international market for economists. As a result, 'good' departments are populated by scholars who produce abstract, formal and theory-driven work. Such departments can be looked at as applied mathematics oriented towards solving self-set problems. 'The economics scholar works for the only coin worth having - our own applause' (Samuelson 1962, p. 18). They do not endeavour to contribute insights to those real life issues that citizens are concerned with, such as unemployment or the destruction of the environment, nor do they offer advice to policy makers.

> *Proposition 3: The economics core remains important where it is not subject to international competition, namely when (a) economics departments can muster protection against*

international competition and (b) economics is located outside economics departments.

Economics departments can be protected from the international competition of economists for jobs for a variety of reasons:

- Language. It should, however, be taken into account that English has become the *lingua franca* in economics (as was Latin in the middle-ages), so that protection arguments only apply to teaching (and not to research), and only for a limited period (languages can be learned).
- Legal barriers, for example, that professors are public servants, and public servants must be nationals.
- Institutional barriers, for example, problems caused by the non-transferability of old age pension rights.
- Rent seeking barriers, where national or even local academic economists refuse to let other economists compete for 'their' jobs.

These barriers to international competition impose costs. Such departments have, on average, less able and less active scholars but only to the extent that they are extrinsically motivated. Intrinsically motivated scholarly productivity is less affected by protectionism. As it is known, scientific research depends to a considerable extent on inner motives. Moreover, a protected sphere may to some extent foster the development of intrinsic motivation.[12] It would thus be unwarranted to jump to the conclusion that protected departments function much worse than those open to competition. Of course, competition increases efficiency in academia *as defined* by the ray standards. However, locally protected economics departments do not need to resort to the signalling standards necessary in international competition, and hence do not produce ray-focused economics. Rather, economists are able to produce locally oriented studies taking into account the respective facts and institutions. Their career and prestige is furthered by enlightening the public on economic and social problems (for example, by writing articles in newspapers for the general public and appearing on radio and TV). They also benefit from offering policy advice and engaging in a political career.

Economists employed by departments outside economics can afford to stick to core economics and to apply it in a useful way to real world issues. As long as these scholars pursue their career, and seek attention and prestige within such departments, they have to attend to problems which other scholars also consider important. In a multi-disciplinary environment the problems are not unlike those that people outside the university system are concerned with.

As the skilful application of core economics yields novel and otherwise disregarded insights compared to other approaches, much of the most stimulating and useful economics is provided by economists in departments of political science, sociology, law or history, often publishing in the respective journals. Indeed, the economic or rational choice approach has proved most useful. An example is the School of Law at Chicago University where Coase (Nobel Prize winner in economics) has been employed, where jurists such as Posner or Easterbrook rely on Public Choice, and where the *Journal of Law and Economics* and *Legal Studies* have published their work. Another example again refers to the University of Chicago: Becker (Nobel Prize winner in economics) is (in addition to economics) a professor of sociology. The sociologist Coleman was the leader of rational choice sociology. Again, the Journal published in that context, *Rationality and Society*, is noteworthy for its stimulating applications of core economics to real world issues. Finally, one may mention Williamson who at Berkeley simultaneously holds a chair in economics and in law.

The situation is quite different if scholars employed in schools outside economics, endeavour to return to an economics faculty. She or he must then strictly adhere to the self-defined problems and standards of economics, that is, one has to contribute and excel in a ray. Schools of Public Policy and of Management in the United States which are designed to deal with real world issues, and who have hired such economists, or have established a department of economics within their school, have made this experience: the economists turn their attention to rigour and formal elegance, neglecting the goals these schools were established for. This seems to have happened to some business schools:

> The primary measure of excellence became publication in discipline-based journals and acceptance by the community of discipline-based scholars, rather

than relevance to practice or contributions to professional education. (Rumelt et al. 1991, p. 17)

Proposition 4: Advice and policy proposal essentially require core economics taught in the first semester, but rarely ever the work produced in ray economics by high flyers and UFOs.

Examples for practical policy proposals essentially based on core economics are vouchers (for example, for schooling or cultural activities), road pricing, environmental incentive instruments (effluent taxes or tradeable licenses), and the negative income tax. They rely on the relative price effect and use it ingeniously to induce people to take external effects into account, to allocate opportunities to those people who value them most highly, and to make work more attractive instead of punishing it. These mechanisms can be applied by first semester students but the real challenge is to take the various institutional conditions into account and to overcome the political resistance of the persons and groups likely to lose by the introduction of these economic policy instruments. A successful application of core economics is thus no trivial task. It does not require advanced ray-economics in the form of rigorous and elegant theorizing.[13] What is needed for that task is a good knowledge of existing conditions (including the legal options) and a considerable amount of common sense aided by experience.[14] To induce young academics to enter ray-economics is thus not costless because such institutional knowledge and experience cannot be gained there. We thus argue that there is a serious trade-off between careers in core or in ray-economics. This trade-off is often refuted by claiming that a member of a ray may easily 'step down' to undertake policy advising. This may well be so, but the quality of the advice offered is accordingly unsatisfactory: it is hardly impossible to deduce any novel and useful policy advice on the basis of a highly sophisticated formal model designed to solve self-defined theoretical problems only.[15] The point is not that the advice would be 'wrong' in any objective sense, but rather that it tends to be trivial for the policy problems at hand, and can as well be given simply on the basis of well-understood core economics.[16,17] The reliance of policy advising on core economics, and the precarious usefulness of ray economics for that purpose, has been acknowledged by many insightful economists knowing both

'worlds'. Thus, Krugman (1995, p. 32) states 'What I learned from
that experience [a policy task at the Central Bank of Portugal] was
the power of very simple economic ideas...', and similarly Stein, the
successful former chairman of the Council of Economic Advisors,
remarked that, 'most of the economics that is usable for advising on
public policy is at about the level of the introductory undergraduate
course' (see Hamilton 1992, p. 62).

2.3   Counterarguments

The position here taken about core and ray-economics, or about first-
year economics *versus* high flyers and UFOs is certainly debatable,
and unlikely to be very popular in the community of ray-economists
in which we normally act, and to which most readers of this chapter
belong. We therefore wish to explicitly deal with the four major
counterarguments against our position, namely

- core and rays will be integrated over time (somewhere in the
  future);
- the international market for economists is a competitive one,
  and therefore the allocation of economists' effort is also
  efficient;
- ray-economics are not devoted to rigour and formal elegance
  as we claim but have increasingly become empirical; and
- surveys have been commissioned to bridge the gaps between
  rays.

Core and rays will be integrated
The development of the science of economics may be seen in a
completely different light. Allowing sufficient time, the various rays
will be joined with each other so that the core of economics is
continually moved outwards and is better and better equipped to
understand the real world. Accordingly, the Figures 2.1. and 2.2
shown should be extended as in Figure 2.3.

The old core (at $t = 0$) is extended to the much larger new one (at
$t = 1$) which embodies all the insights included in the various rays.
The new core forms the basis for new rays which after some time
produce a yet larger core.

Figure 2.3   Optimistic, ray-integrative conception of economics

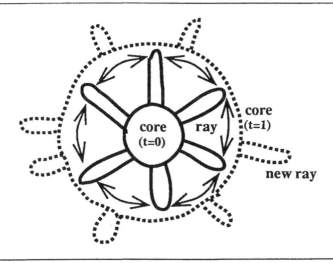

Some might even argue that Figures 2.1 and 2.2 were wrong and that economics is better seen as a tyre filled with (useful!) air and rolling quickly (Figure 2.4). The rays are intimately connected with each other, interchanging their insights quickly.

Figure 2.4 The highly optimistic tyre conception of economics

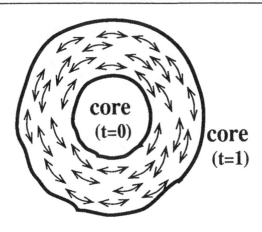

The suggestion of a continually increasing core on the basis of the rays must be taken seriously: does not a graduate of economics know much more today than a generation ago, and did not that generation know more than the preceding one? This is an almost philosophical question. What is certainly true is that they know more and better techniques - but at the same time it must be conceded that they know less history and institutional facts. Whether they are better equipped to understand and integrate reality, and to make sensible policy proposals, is not *a priori* clear.

We are sceptical whether the extension of the core as illustrated by Figures 2.3 and 2.4 is really happening in such a harmonious way. It could be asked whether we have sufficient time to overcome the pressing problems of our generation (for example, unemployment or old age pensions) by integrating rays. Would it not be preferable to have contributions based on the existing core, rather than to perhaps vainly hope that a much superior solution will be possible on the basis of a future core? Even more fundamentally, it can be questioned whether the various rays will really be connected with each other in the future. Here, normative appeals and wishful thinking should be distinguished carefully.[18]

Figure 2.5   Extending the core is risky

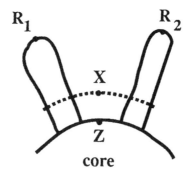

Consider Figure 2.5. To try to bridge the gap between two rays (R_1 and R_2) is extremely risky. Consider a young scholar who manages to provide work that positions her at point X. The knowledge generated is clearly superior to the one attainable solely on the basis of core economics (point Z). The crucial point is that the evaluation of the quality of that research is undertaken by 'good' scholars (according to the standards in economics). This means that the referees of journals or other scientific achievements (for example, referring to decisions about grants) are located somewhere on or near the tip of a ray (see Hamermesh 1994). Being highly specialized, they typically state that they value the integrative efforts of the scholar concerned, but that the contribution at X is, of course, by far not as good as some in their respective ray. They *generally* favour the work but confess that they are unable to judge it from a general perspective, and further add that from their own scientific point of view it is not up to the standards.

To try to bridge the gap between rays thus is a risky strategy where a failure, and therewith the end of the academic career, is very likely. Success depends on two rare conditions. One is that one tries to establish a new ray but this requires the right time and extraordinary capacities. Indeed, it is successfully achieved by the most able scholars only few of whom (a long time afterwards) are rewarded by a Nobel Prize. Pertinent examples are North and Fogel (new economic history), Arrow and Buchanan (public choice), or Becker (non-market economics). A second possibility for achieving success is to first accumulate a reputation by working in one particular ray, and then to try to bridge rays only later. Examples would be Akerlof who worked in growth theory and then switched to psychological economics, or Baumol and Peacock who started cultural economics. However, even scholars of that calibre find it exceedingly difficult to be successful with that strategy as the history of rejected articles shows (Gans and Shepard 1994). Both strategies, even if they were successful in the long run, require considerable time - and time is a costly resource in an environment of ray-economics where quick publication and citation results are required.

To undertake an integrative strategy is even more risky when a bridge to another discipline is to be established. To exploit economic orthodoxy to the fullest is good advice given to young economists embarking on an academic career. This strategy is beneficial to economics in so far as inconsistencies between methodologies (for example, between economics based on methodological individualism and systems theory based on a holistic approach) are prevented. It has, however, negative consequences when the orthodox economic approach is used until its marginal productivity is close to, or at zero. In that case more insights would be created by equalizing marginal productivity of each approach which means not over-extending the use of a particular discipline. Young scholars are, of course, not interested in these 'social' benefits (that is, the fate of economics as a whole) but pursue their private benefits that indicate clearly that the expected benefits of risk neutral or risk averse young academics is to embark on a ray.[19] Only uninformed and naive, or highly risk loving, or rather incompetent or lazy ones (who are unlikely to be successful in any ray) find it privately advantageous to undertake interdisciplinary or interray research.

Competitive markets are optimal
The international market for economists is competitive, and competition produces Pareto-optimal (efficient) results, provided the necessary conditions are met. Even if the conditions do not fully apply, competition is considered to be healthy by economists, and certainly preferable to alternative allocation mechanisms. Hence - so it is argued - the market for economists produces the socially most desired output, and the reservations raised in this chapter are unfounded.

We agree with the observation that the international market for economists has become more competitive (and we predict that this development will intensify; see section 2.4 below). But we point out that there is a basic asymmetry of information on the international market for economists which produces a systematic distortion of outcomes and drives the competitive process in a non-optimal direction. The basic informational asymmetry is due to the great uncertainty existing in a largely anonymous international market. It is difficult or impossible to judge the content of research as the knowledge about the underlying facts and institutions is seriously incomplete or missing among the evaluators based in another country or continent. Hence technical aspects - rigour and formal elegance - are judged. Young academics are induced to produce research in which they excel on this regard. The result is an aggregate research output which is systematically distorted in favour of abstract work, and against research dealing with real-life issues.

Another reason why the competitive international market for economists does not produce an optimal outcome is due to the fact that demand and supply for research output are not independent as the suppliers (the economists producing research) at the same time largely determine demand (they define what research is by defining it within their own community). The requirement that demanders and suppliers are independent actors reacting to a price is violated so that no optimal output can be expected. The situation is similar to the market for medical care where the doctors as suppliers to a large extent determine the demand by the patients.

Modern economics is empirical

Recent studies have come to the conclusion that the share of 'empirical' papers has increased over the last 30 years, but that this trend came to an end in the 1980s (T. Morgan 1988, Figlio 1994). The question is, of course, what 'empirical' means in this context. Our contention is that due to the evaluation standards in international economics and the refereeing system going with it, articles published in major mainstream journals tend to be abstract and formal, dealing with well-defined theoretical issues. This also applies to 'empirical' studies in the form of econometric estimates of theoretical models whose major emphasis lies on estimation technique.[20] 'Empirical' research is just another way to exhibit one's technical competence, and thus to meet the profession's self-defined standards.[21] The typical author does not even claim to present a balanced picture of empirical reality, including the institutional background, but is interested in showing the intricacies of a particular econometric technique. This interpretation is shared by Solow who states that 'many empirical papers seem more like virtuoso finger exercise than anything else' (quoted by Lazonick 1991, p. 348).

The need to evaluate the research of economists in the international market also systematically distorts the kind of data used. The safest way to proceed is to use the data established scholars have used before for the same kind of technical (econometric) exercise.[22] Another acceptable way to proceed is to simply use official statistics. In both cases the international referees can concentrate on the theoretical and empirical techniques employed. This means, however, that economic analysis is undertaken on the basis of a consensual statistical 'reality' which is rarely challenged.

Data generated on the basis of official statistics, for example, by constructing indices, is already tricky in the international market because the referees find it costly to evaluate such rather nitty-gritty transformations.[23] To collect data oneself does not only cost much time and effort (and is therefore not a good choice for young scholars who have to publish quickly) but it is also extremely difficult to evaluate by a referee not intimately connected with the respective economy and period. This is a clear disadvantage in the international market. Moreover, the collector of data has possibilities to 'massage' the data by, for example, leaving out outlayers (without explicitly saying so) or even to falsify data. Because of such uncertainties, international referees much prefer to evaluate the analytical and econometric techniques used to deal with well-established data because he or she feels competent to do so, and does not require specific institutional and historical knowledge. Hence, there are few incentives especially for young researchers to collect new data, and the data that have been newly collected are not subjected to a similar degree of critical analysis as are the formal aspects of economics. As a result, rather bad data may survive for a considerable time, and the econometric techniques are used to explain a chimera.

It might be argued that the rise of experimental economics (see, for example, Kagel and Roth 1995) presents clear contrary evidence against our proposition. After all, experiments are undertaken exactly to produce new data under controlled conditions. Here is indeed a weak spot in this movement which so far has mainly been discussed in the natural sciences, but very little in experimental economics. In principle, the results of an experiment can be made up, or at least massaged by, for example, excluding experimental runs with awkward results. Our contention is not that this happens to any large degree or even that it has ever happened in experimental economics, but only that a referee has hardly the possibility to really check. In view of this difficulty, the international economics community has responded in various ways:

- the set-up of the experiments must be exactly described in publications in order to facilitate replication;
- the experimenters have established a rather closely-knit network of personal contacts in order to informally monitor each other and to establish reputations; and
- standard experiments have received great prominence (the Prisoner's Dilemma Game, and more recently the Ultimatum Game) which eases the burden of evaluation. It is easier to compare a new experiment to an already existing set of standard experiments.

In particular the last two responses are the prerequisites for a ray, which indeed experimental economics is today. The scholars in this ray mainly or even exclusively relate to and quote each other, they engage in marginal adjustments within the cannon of experiments deemed acceptable by them, and they deal to a large degree with self-defined technical and theoretical problems while the content increasingly loses importance.[24]

Surveys bridge the gap
Could it not be argued that the economics community has responded to the gaps existing between rays by commissioning evaluative surveys of existing knowledge?

This argument is not without merit as there are *some* surveys that try to link the developments of various, or at least two rays. However, most surveys have exactly the opposite function, namely to highlight, establish and advertise a given ray in the general economics community.[25] Not rarely, such surveys seek to pull together the various threads *within* a ray, and do not endeavour to transgress the ray they survey. Almost never do they seriously integrate knowledge from the other social sciences.[26] But what about *surveys* that are commissioned to deal with a policy issue such as unemployment? One would think that the authors are *forced* to go beyond the abstract and technically-oriented model building and must seriously deal with the question of what economics as a social science is able to contribute. We contend that this is not normally the case because the writers of surveys are subject to the need for evaluation by referees who look at rigour and formal elegance but are not really interested in improving economic policy. Consider, by way of example, the recent survey published in the *Journal of Economic Literature* on 'European Unemployment'. The author (Bean 1994) is a well-respected scholar who behaves as predicted, namely by essentially staying within the discourse among economists who have defined what they consider to be 'interesting' issues. Bean does refer to some policy consequences: after about 40 pages of treating theories he deals on half a page (p. 615) with policy consequences. However, these are not at all up to the quality standard of the previous theory-oriented part. He states that flexibility on the labour market would be helpful, as well as an active labour market policy as in Sweden (p. 615). While the first suggestion is rather trivial and known to everyone, the second has proved to be most doubtful (Sweden has currently an unemployment rate of 8.8 per cent). While the discussion of the theories was precise and rigorous, the policy conclusions are unspecific, short, not backed by empirical analysis, and moreover rather unconnected to the wealth of theories previously expounded at length. This is, of course, not because Bean is incompetent but rather because he is competent according to economists' self-defined standard. It should be added that Bean makes another policy proposal, namely to employ vouchers in the labour market (p. 615). Though not exactly new (it is a rather stereotype proposal economists are fond of making), only five lines are devoted to it so that it is not discussed in any serious way. While vouchers are interesting, the major problem is how to apply them precisely, and how to get them accepted in the political process.

2.4   Prospects for the Future

Increasing competition
The market for economists is almost certainly going to be more competitive in the future than it was in the past. As a by-product of the European unification, economists have organized themselves at the European level (the European Economic Association), and have established joint graduate programs (as, for example, between the Universities of Bonn, Louvain and LSE). At the same time the interaction between Europe and North America has further increased. Many American scholars now teach full-time or part-time in Europe,

as well as European scholars in America. The same applies for students. At the research level, the interaction is even more intensive; it is hardly possible to see any differences between the two continents.

All this is in marked contrast to the situation in the past where economists' jobs, education and research markets were defined according to nations and when it was rare that a scholar of another country was accepted as a professor.[27]

Following our proposition, we expect that the formation of an all-European market for economists (in particular among the EU-member states) and its increased integration with the North American market leads to three major consequences:

- rays will become more important;
- economics departments will increasingly be a part of applied mathematics; and
- economics will flourish in other faculties.

Rays will become more important

The intensified competition among economists induces them to adjust to the conditions in the market. To be successful they have to produce rigorous and formally elegant work on self-defined theoretical problems. There will be more rays, that is, specialization is expected to go even further, and these rays will play an even larger role compared to the core.[28] This development will be reflected in the foundation of increasingly differentiated journals and associations.[29] At the same time this means that economics increasingly takes place outside the core, and that the compactness which characterized economics compared to the other social sciences is impaired.

Economics departments will increasingly be a part of applied mathematics

As a reaction to the more intensive competition economics departments will have to follow the internationally established standards. Only scholars excelling in rigour and formalism will be appointed as professors while those mainly interested in content and explaining real life issues have little chance in future economics departments. As students are well aware that an education in ray economics is far from useful to get a job outside economics departments, only few will rationally decide to go beyond core economics and to enter graduate school. In the United States (at the leading universities and even at lower ranked schools) the economists' market has been competitive for a long time, and economics departments thus are strongly ray focused. As a consequence, very few Americans choose to take up graduate studies in economics. At many universities, graduate economics schools can only survive because they are populated by Asian and European students.[30] For them an education in ray economics may be profitable because a competitive market among economists is only gradually emerging, and the positions are increasingly occupied by economists meeting the international standards of rigour and formal elegance. Once the market among economists is established, graduate education will almost exclusively be to cater for the reinvestment demand of economics departments. If these arguments are correct, economics departments will *survive*, but will be *small*.

In economics departments dominated by ray economics policy advising will play a small role. It is not considered part of scientific activities as its output is not reflected in publications in accepted (refereed) journals and in citations. This trend is already visible; there is circumstantial evidence that advice pertaining to practical economic policy making is increasingly not sought from members of economics departments but from outside. The only members of such departments who can afford to 'waste' time on advising are those who made it and are outside the rat race. However, as we pointed out above, the advice on economic policy will either be of a technical nature and/or on the level of first semester economics.[31]

Economics will flourish in other faculties

Traditional economics departments where the professors cater for local demands, for general economic erudition and policy advice will largely vanish because the opening up of all markets makes it impossible to establish artificial barriers to entry. The natural barriers of language are due to evaporate because English will become the *lingua franca* of an increasingly large part of the world.

Economists interested in real life issues and policy problems will be found in faculties of law, business, political science, sociology, psychology, history and policy science. They apply rational choice analysis of core economics and will be well-known outside academia if they do so successfully. (They may even produce bestsellers.) However, this position is lost if the disciplines in which such economists are hosted follow the same development as economics departments. If they do so on the basis of ray economics they will similarly lose outside importance and will merge with economics departments as a further small part of applied mathematics. If they embark on rays based on different methodologies (such as systems theory), the economists will be forced out. Whether the disciplines mentioned above will increasingly value technique over content depends on the extent of international competition of the respective markets for scholars.

2.5   Are there Endogenous Limits?

The present and future development of economics as here portrayed, if indeed correct and shared by others, might be expected to lead to corrective reactions by those most negatively affected. One group is 'the public' which no longer derives any visible benefits from the economics departments. As far as the general population is concerned, it can at best be considered to be a latent group about whose component members they have little or no interest in complaining as the outcome is a public good. The government and organized groups do not really depend on economics departments as they can turn to economists in other faculties as well as to other social sciences. Hence, no reaction from the public is likely to be forthcoming.

A group which is potentially much more strongly affected are the (future) students of economics who, when educated in ray economics even at the undergraduate level, will find it difficult to find a job. But this group is also unlikely to change the course. First, potential future economics students do not have an incentive, nor the insights or influence (they are youngsters in schools), to become active. Second, the job situation is not hopeless because - at least outside North America - the existing stock of professors is still to be filled up with economists trained in rays. It is a well-known psychological bias already extensively commented on by Adam Smith, and empirically well supported (Weinstein 1980) that prospective entrants into an occupation or job systematically overrate the probability of being successful. So even if there are relatively few professional jobs to be filled in the future, any particular potential economics graduate believes to be among the chosen few, and therefore sees little reason to redress economics teaching to the study of real world issues.

This leaves a third group which might be concerned about the sketched future development of economics, the scholars having a job in an economics department. As everywhere, change will be resisted, which is strengthened by the fact that most professors have tenure so that they are to a large extent isolated from market developments (see Alchian 1977). Those educated in the tradition that rigour and formal elegance mainly matter, have little reason to redress the balance because they would be robbed of a significant share of the human capital they accumulated with much effort. In addition to those obvious material interests they may also be subject to the drive to reduce cognitive dissonance by overvaluing the training received in the past. Only professors who have either had a broader education or who are so superior that they have acquired a broader knowledge of economics and the social sciences (good examples are Solow and Arrow, but there are many others) will want to seriously put into question the course of their own departments. They are joined by university administrators who are forced to compare the future development of various departments. Both these unorthodox professors and university administrators cannot fail to see some signs speaking against ray-economics. One is the falling number of economics students compared, for example, to management (business) and law, as well as the difficulty in finding satisfactory and well paid jobs outside academia.[32] Whether these two groups are able to change the course of events depends strongly on institutional conditions. Private universities which depend on satisfying students' preferences are more likely to redress the balance in favour of core economics which means that the ray oriented departments of economics will shrink. State universities, especially of the European type, depend less directly on future job opportunities of students, and have a stronger tenure security for professors, so that less rapid change is likely to occur. As a larger share of American universities are private (especially the top ones) this would mean that the departments of economics will shrink more quickly in North America than in Europe.

2.6 Changing the Evaluation: From PC to PEP

Our analysis and our predictions are based on the notion that the increased internationalization of the market for economists requires an efficient and reasonably objective standard for evaluating the performance of individual economists. For the reasons outlined, the quality evaluation hinges on rigour and formal elegance aspects which are reflected in journal publications refereed by other economists, and their impact on the professional discussion, i.e. citations. But it is exactly due to this mechanism that economic research is strongly distorted away from analysing real world issues, and towards the abstract analysis of self-defined problems.

Why should this evaluation not be broadened by going beyond 'Publications and Citations' (PC) to a more general 'Professional Evaluation Procedure' (PEP)? Economists' quality might be judged along three major dimensions (Table 2.1).

Table 2.1   Dimensions of economist quality (PEP-index)

Research	publications and citations, this is the PC-yardstick now employed.
Social activities	(a) in the public sector, either as a member of government or as a public official; (b) in the various parliaments, be they central, provincial or local (and possible the functions such as president of the finance committee); (c) as advisers in the various economic councils such as the 'sachverständigenrat'.
Academic management	University rector, faculty dean, or department chairperson.

The information contained in these three dimensions can be condensed in the *PEP-Index*. The construction and use of the PEP-Index is, however, faced with serious problems. First, the aspects included are only partial, and it is easy to think of activities which should also be included. Why should, for instance, advising firms or interest groups not be one of the qualities of an economist (and not only of a business economist) worth taking into account? And why should we stop with advising? Should not actual business activities also be included? And if so, why not volunteer work? From this it is only a minor step to also incorporate artistic and sports activities. The point is clear: It is difficult or even impossible to find a set of activities which would command wide consensus. This is in marked contrast to publications and citations where corresponding conventions have emerged. Moreover, does it make sense to define a successful business person (or sportsperson) to be a good academic simply because the distinction between advising and academia is blurred? Second, the PEP-Index is most difficult to compare over different periods and countries. In one country, for instance, the president of the parliamentary finance committee or the university rector may have enormous power, and in another country it may just be a nice, but meaningless title. Moreover, occupying a position does not mean that one does it well.

The first two difficulties are serious (and more serious than in the case of the currently used - P or C - indices) but could, at least in principle, be overcome by a standardization system. The third difficulty, however, is fundamental. The PEP-Index is made up of three different dimensions, and there is no objective way to aggregate them. There exists no readily available market system which determines the relative prices, or weights, of the three dimensions. Depending on the weights used, many different outcomes can be produced. If the PC part is given large weight, the American economists are without any doubt on top (and that is exactly what Portes 1987, p. 1220 states when he asks 'whether there is now any economics outside and independent of the United States?'). But if sufficient weight is given to jobs in government, it is the Dutch and the Spanish economists who are top (as we have argued in Frey and Eichenberger 1993). Depending on one's purpose and interests, the convenient weight will be chosen, and - as scientific research on preference aggregation has made abundantly clear (reaching back to Black 1948 and Arrow 1951, see Sen 1970) - there is *no* logically consistent way of performing such an aggregation in a world of heterogeneous preferences. It is, of course, possible to resort to a dictatorial solution by *imposing* a system of weights, for example, via an international standardization agreement. However, such a PEP-Index would have little use.

As the construction of a meaningful single PEP-Index seems to be impossible, one could rely on several PEP-indicators mirroring the various dimensions of performance. This, however, does not solve the aggregation problem; it only makes the subjectivity of aggregation more explicit. The situation is not quite unlike the efforts with national accounting. As long as the convention was to essentially use market weights to aggregate the individual goods and services to national income, there were little problems. (The fact that government activity is measured by input rather than by output is conveniently overlooked.) But the extension to include environmental damages as well as the exhaustion of natural resources has been much more difficult (even if undertaken by the World Bank), and is used only under very special circumstances. The situation with the PEP-Index is more serious, not least because individual scholars are personally and strongly affected.

We are forced to conclude that while extending the basis of evaluation of economists would be desirable and important, a PEP-Index certainly does not provide a rough and ready solution. It is rather the other way around. If the institutional conditions have changed such that scholars are not mainly evaluated on the basis of rigour and formal elegance, then it is more likely that a consensus on a standardized PEP-Index may emerge.

2.7 Conclusions

The analysis of the *status quo* and of future developments here presented are certainly evaluated quite differently according to the person and her or his interests:

- Persons interested in economics as an institution will find our analysis frightening as we predict that the departments of economics will shrink to a small size.
- Persons only interested in an economics conforming to the rigour and formal elegance of the natural sciences (especially mathematics) will welcome this development toward a 'real' science with a few chosen students.
- Persons interested in the subject and content of economics as a social science and hence in core economics will deplore the disappearance of economics departments as a relevant social unit but will be consoled by economics flourishing in other disciplines.

Our analysis and predictions are therefore neither pessimistic nor optimistic. We have not tried to hide our own preferences. We consider ourselves members of the third group. We consider core economics to be an invaluable contribution to the social sciences, and we firmly believe that it is both strict and flexible enough to be further developed and amended by insights from other disciplines. Economics so understood is great.

Notes

We thank Felix Oberholzer-Gee and Richard Portes for helpful comments.
1. In political science the economic approach is known as 'Public Choice', in sociology as 'Rational Choice', in Law as 'Law and Economics', in international relations as 'International Political Economy', in criminology as the 'Economic Approach to Crime', in history as 'New Economic History' and 'Cliometrics' (see, for examples Becker 1976, McKenzie and Tullock 1975, Frey 1992).
2. For related work on economics and the economic profession, see, for example, Colander and Klamer (1987), Colander (1989), Klamer and Colander (1990), Baumol (1995), Buchanan (1995), Eggertsson (1995), and Frech (1995).
3. Indeed, one of the present authors has been engaged in rather extensive empirical studies dealing with the issue. They replicate and extend a study for the US (Kearl et al. 1979) to Europe: Frey et al. (1982) to Switzerland, Schneider et al. (1983) to Germany, Pommerehne et al. (1983) to Austria, Bobe and Etchegoyen (1981) to France. The results were compared in Frey et al. (1984) and Pommerehne et al. (1984). Further replications have thereafter been undertaken, for example, for the United Kingdom by Ricketts and Shoesmith (1990) and for the US by Alston et al. (1992).

4. Many articles are never read by anybody beyond the journal editor (perhaps) and his referees. Even more are never ever quoted.
5. 'It is a fact of life that trained economists find it very difficult to see the obvious unless it has been encapsulated in a clear formal model' (Krugman 1995, p.43). It is tempting to compare ray-economics to scholastic as well as to some modern parts of philosophy of which Feyerabend (1995, p. 197) says: 'Ihr seid wie die Gelehrten im Mittelalter ... Die verstanden auch nur, was sie zuvor ins Lateinische übersetzt hatten' (You are like the medieval scientists who could only understand what they had just translated into Latin).
6. It is well possible to write a whole book on 'The Economics of the Family' (Cigno 1991) without integrating any empirical facts about the family and without consulting the (huge) literature on the family offered by the other social sciences. This sad fact can be generalized. As a consequence, only 3 per cent of young American economists perceive 'having a thorough knowledge of the economy' to be 'very important' for professional success, while 65 per cent think 'being smart in the sense of being good at problem solving' and 57 per cent believe that 'excellence in mathematics' is very important (see Colander and Klamer 1987, p. 100, or Klamer and Colander 1990, p. 18). Thus, Bergman (1989) rightly asks the questions 'Why Do Economists Know so Little about the Economy?' and Fisher (1989, p. 123) bluntly writes:

    > There is a strong tendency for even the best practitioners to concentrate on the analytically interesting questions rather than on the ones that really matter. The result is often a perfectly fascinating piece of analysis. But so long as that tendency continues, those analyses will remain merely games economists play.

    See with similar statements Kolm (1988), Colander (1991) and Mayer (1993).
7. In the words of three well known business scholars: 'Less and less concerned with empiricism, economics became increasingly concerned with working out the internal logic of its theoretical structure and less concerned with discussing real institutions' (Rumelt et al. 1991, p. 17).
8. An example (according to Drèze 1995, p. 119-20) are the theories of incentive compatibility.
9. Or in Phelps' (1995, p. 103) words: 'a science develops momentum in a certain line of analysis, ... something like an industry develops with its accumulated conventions and standards'.
10. The dominant position of Americans in the world market of economists is documented in Frey and Pommerehne (1988a) by counting citations. See also Kirman and Dahl (1994, pp. 514-17).
11. One may even speak of a fundamental 'Unentscheidbarkeits-Theorem' (Holub 1989). The issue is also extensively discussed in Frey and Eichenberger (1992 and 1993).
12. The (often destructive) influence of extrinsic incentives on intrinsic motivations is extensively analysed in Frey (1997a and 1997b).

13. In Osterloh, Grand and Tiemann's (1994) terminology one needs not only *modelling* (that is, the isolation of a few key variables whose interactions are examined in depth; they focus on strong links, see Mayer 1993) but also *mapping* (that is, the use of different models from different disciplinary views, thus trying to map the diversity inherent in concrete situations).

14. 'once you've seen the primitive nature of real policy discussion, you start to wonder whether third-order conditions and likelihood-tests can really matter' (Krugman 1995, p. 35).

15. An extensive account on the gap between academic (ray) economics taught at universities and the economic concepts that are useful in policy advising is given by Harberger (1993). He openly declares on p. 12: 'I feel quite safe in stating that we do not have, in the United States, either the amount or the kind of training that is needed for our profession to make its appropriate contribution to our society's decision-making processes'.

16. An example is sealed bid second price auctions. Many academic economists believe them to be a genuine economic invention and their application to privatization schemes and public tenders to be a major success of ray economics. However, this alleged economic invention has been the standard mechanism (for written offers) in art and collectibles auctions for centuries (see, for example, *The New Palgrave*, 1987, vol. 1, 139f.), and its favourable properties are known to (almost) all art sellers and buyers.

17. Defenders of the real-life relevance of ray economics might argue that core economics can only be well understood if the respective person has done more advanced economics. This argument is not without merit. However, it should be weighted against the additional insights gained by learning about the relevant institutional conditions, and gaining knowledge about how to make economic ideas acceptable in the economic policy process.

18. An example is the official speeches by the presidents of the American Economic Association at the yearly meetings. These chosen scholars use to urge their co-economists to do more reality oriented and integrative work. The majority of younger economists listen politely, but with their career in mind return home not changing one bit their effort to excel in ray economics.

19. Phelps (1995, p. 103) offers this advice: 'a researcher can normally expect to maximize citations by correcting or building upon an established or ongoing research programme ... not by centering into an area where there are few or no citations to begin with'.

20. An example is the use of cointegration analysis which can be applied to a large number of issues. The first author as editor of a professional journal (*Kyklos*) has received virtually dozens of papers where this new estimation technique has been applied, and where the respective authors obviously had little, or no interest, in the subject the technique has been applied to. This can be generalized: 'formal empirical work ... has had almost no influence on serious thinking about substantive as opposed to methodological questions' (Summers 1991, p. 129).

21. The following abstract announcing a contribution on 'Applied Economics' to the European Economic Association Conference in Prague in 1995 is quite typical: 'Using a translog cost functional form a formal operational model with an adjustment process according to a first-order autoregressive scheme is presented that allows the simultaneous determination of factor demands and of technological change in an input-output system' (Saturday, Sept. 2, Section C9). The authors do not bother to even hint at any substantive problem.

22. The Summers and Heston (1991) data on real national income for more than 130 nations are a good example. They are generally considered the 'correct' ones and are used as a matter of course by the scholars participating in cross-country growth research (for example, Levine and Renelt 1992) but few would seriously argue that they are really good and could not be improved upon.

23. For instance the Scully (1992) index on political and economic liberties, or Gastil's (1989) freedom index.

24. This does not say that experimental economics is not able to produce new insights which help us to understand better the world we live in. On the contrary, we believe that the approach which we have ourselves used, is most helpful. See for example, Bohnet and Frey (1995), Frey and Bohnet (1995), Eichenberger and Oberholzer (1995).

25. We have already mentioned Hahn and Mathew's (1964) growth survey; Harcourt's (1972) and Blaug's (1975) surveys on the Cambridge Capital Controversy. Another more recent example is Throsby's (1994) survey on cultural economics.

26. If other disciplines are considered this is normally done on the methodological level, stating, for example, that the other social sciences dealing with the same issues are not based on methodological individualism. But normally the surveys leave it at that.

27. An exception has been between Germany, Austria and Switzerland where an open market for German speaking professors has always existed.

28. To illustrate with an example: already today, research on field experiments and on laboratory experiments in economics is almost totally separated, that is, there are hardly any cross references, not even in surveys (for evidence see Frey and Bohnet, 1996). We expect that within laboratory economics there will be rays on labour, on values and fairness, on markets, and on decision making (dilemmata) experiments. These divisions are already visible today. In this context Solow (1967, p. 101) warns 'little-thinking can easily degenerate into mini-thinking or even into hardly any thinking at all'.

29. Even in a field which most professional economists have never even heard about, such as the economics of art, there are several specialized journals: *The Journal of Cultural Economics, Empirical Studies in the Arts,* and *Economia della Cultura.* In a better known field such as public choice there are even more specialized journals, for example, *Public Choice, Constitutional Political Economy, Economia delle Scelte Pubbliche, Politics and Economics, European Journal of Political Economy, Social Choice and Welfare,* and so on.

30. For the huge share of foreign students in Doctoral programmes in the US see, for example, Hansen (1991).

31. Examples are Arrow and Solow who co-chaired a panel evaluating the contingent valuation approach (Arrow, Solow et al. 1993). In that case, the advice was rather basic (how to undertake a useful survey), certainly not going beyond core economics.

32. See Krueger et al. (1991) and Towse and Blaug (1990). If these findings hold, we expect a declining relative wage of economics graduates compared to, for example, lawyers and MBAs. However, as far as we know there exists no serious empirical evidence concerning this prediction.

3. Users and Abusers of Economic Research

Richard Portes

Let me start with a question. Are there no examples of areas where economics demonstrably does influence public and private sector decision making? Contrary to Frey and Eichenberger in the previous Chapter, I suggest that many such examples exist. To name just a few: EMU, NAFTA, corporate governance, the Uruguay round, deregulation and privatization, Central Bank independence, trade policy reform in less developed countries, reducing financial repression, competition policy, foreign direct investment. These subjects are all areas where economics and economists have made easily identifiable contributions. And note: much of it is clearly not core economics.

These contributions are not necessarily only in a maximizing, individual, optimizing framework, with no regard for social institutions or social interactions. That framework is often used by economists, but a lot of research on, for example, strategic interaction does not limit itself to that sort of paradigm. Moreover, these contributions meet the market test. People in industry, finance, Central Banks, international organizations and even government departments are actually willing to pay for economic research. Have they been conned? I do not think so.

I have devoted a lot of my time and effort over the past fifteen years to policy-related research, much of which Frey and Eichenberger find unattractive and even perhaps dangerous. And I have sought to get a wide range of economists involved in analysing economic policy issues. Aiming at economists that are first class by the standard professional criteria, the goal has been to get the 'stars'

49

to deal with economic policy. This comes down to the application of first-class technique to policy research.

For any of Frey and Eichenberger's anecdotes and examples one can provide many counterexamples. They fear that the 'Americanization' of professional standards is leading to the dominance of irrelevant high theory. But most of the top American economists have been involved in applied and policy-related work. Stiglitz, for example, did - like many of us - mainly do theory at the beginning. However, he also went to an Indian village to study rural credit markets, and that is how he learned about moral hazard. And if you read, for example, Akerlof's 1984 paper on the 'market for lemons' you will discover that Stiglitz was not alone in that regard. Indeed, good economics involves both thorough knowledge of theory and sophisticated application.

This is why academic economists do not give their professional rewards only to those who produce minor variations on proofs of abstract theorems. Even core journals publish research on unemployment, the causes of growth, inequality, economic transformation in Eastern Europe, or the costs and benefits of economic integration. The *Brookings Papers on Economic Activity* ranks highly on citations and impact factor. And *Economic Policy* is a journal which has successfully brought in the young 'stars' who are very able in straight professional activity.

A specific counterexample: sovereign debt
Let me illustrate some of these points with a recent project on orderly workouts for sovereign debtors. That research analysed proposed procedures for dealing with 'Mexico-style' debt crises. I was involved, and I had to learn a lot of economics I did not know, in particular the economics of bankruptcy, an area which has been quite popular among theorists in the past several years. A fresh look at bankruptcy theory was necessary to understand the issues involved and to assess the validity of analogies between domestic bankruptcy laws and the management of international insolvency and illiquidity. For example, the value of the underlying asset which is so important when dealing with corporate bankruptcy (because there is a market test) does not operate in the international context. Fairly sophisticated

theory is necessary to understand how you can deal with the case of an apparently bankrupt sovereign government.

And now I ask myself: is that core economics? Do we teach that in the first year undergraduate course? To apply it properly, certainly not. And I ask myself: is the bankruptcy theory that has developed so much over the past ten years just the irrelevant speculation of high-powered academics? Again, certainly not.

This project on orderly workouts for sovereign debtors also involved serious interdisciplinary work, with major inputs from an economic historian and from two international lawyers. This interdisciplinary approach was generated by the problem. The issue was not constructed so as to bring in some economists, some lawyers, some sociologists and so on. Indeed those who are trying to force interdisciplinary research on us artificially do not understand how research is actually being done.

3.1   Why Are Economists Abused?

So much for the good news. I cannot help but feel that the profession is being wrongly abused for our supposed lack of usefulness and relevance to the real world.

Let us look in somewhat more detail at some of the arguments that are often put forward:

- the perceived irrelevance of (formal) economic theory and econometrics;
- the apparent disagreement among economists; and
- the failure in forecasting.

Irrelevance
It is true that an uncomfortably high proportion of the informed public believes that much of economic theory and econometrics does not and cannot deal with everyday issues that confront them in their work or in the press. Partly they are right, but partly the problem is that economics is not simple. Indeed, much economic analysis is often counterintuitive. Comparative advantage, for example, is difficult to explain to beginning students and even more difficult for those who are actually involved in policy.

It is true that the users themselves (the business community, government departments, politicians) do not use sophisticated economics in that sense. It is also true that theoretical advances do not immediately imply new policies. As Malinvaud (1995) points out, economists do not produce exploitable innovations (we do not make 'discoveries'), and it is such innovations that typically interest business people. Again, this supposed irrelevance of academic economics may be a matter of perception, since much of today's frontier research ultimately becomes the basic concepts of tomorrow - consider, for example, work on expectations, credibility, time inconsistency, or the NAIRU (the non-accelerating inflation rate of unemployment). Moreover, we should be careful not to equate applied economics to policy analysis. Policy analysis is one part of applied economics, but we are also simply trying to understand how economies work. That kind of applied economics has a value in itself outside of government or international organizations.

In the United Kingdom economists have been criticized (see, for example, Hutton and Couglan 1995, Ormerod 1994) for the inappropriateness and even bias of conventional economics. In France, the December 1995 issue of *Le Monde Diplomatique* blames Anglo-Saxon *libre échangisme* and deregulation for social unrest, indeed for all social problems including social exclusion. Now you may want to argue that this is a political mood rather than informed criticism of economics as such. Falling student numbers in economics are blamed on the irrelevance of economics and its mathematical nature.

But the supposed increasing irrelevance of academic economics is simply false. When used properly, mathematical models and econometric techniques essentially enable us to handle more complexity in economic behaviour and in the data. Experimental economics is a growing area that allows us to find how individuals actually behave, and it is published by core journals. We are now coming to grips with strategic interaction and learning behaviour. We can simulate the effects of changes in taxes, incentives and incomes. We can even explain with formal modelling some counterintuitive results: for example, economic policies that could make everyone better off may nevertheless not be popular in a democratic society, whereas bad economic policies may yield short-term electoral benefits.

In fact, economists provide the basic framework for policy analysis, as suggested for example by the pioneering work of Tinbergen: the framework of means and ends, of instruments and targets, the distinction between efficiency and equity, the notion of opportunity costs and trade-offs, the proper use of quantitative data. Economists can contribute with all these tools to policy analysis.

Disagreement

It is of course true that there is apparent disagreement among academic economists. Economists like an argument, and the economic journalists who often act as the policy maker's filter for academic research naturally like controversy. Economists disagreeing on something is a story, while economists agreeing on something is no news. Journalists like sound bites, and they like topics that lend themselves to (over-) simplification. But this is surely not fundamental disagreement about the basic analytical structure of our field.

Over a wide range, there is agreement about the underlying framework, even where there may be schools. On macroeconomic policy, for example, a conservative 'monetarist' supply-side economist can communicate with a social-democrat 'Keynesian' on the basis of shared underlying assumptions, and they can understand each other although they do not agree. The point is that they would actually know (and agree on) what kind of data would confirm or invalidate a proposition. And much of what appears to be the disagreement comes simply from our *métier* of exhibiting trade-offs. When you have different trade-offs, you also have different weights that can be attached to the outcomes.

In some respects there may be excessive agreement and solidarity within the discipline. The imperialism of economics with respect to other social sciences is a problem. The ambition of economists to use their models and framework on any variety of social data can of course go too far, and our use of professional jargon can have the effect of excluding non-economists from discussions of problems that do enter their domains as well as ours. This imperialist attitude is one of the reasons why some of our social science colleagues get upset with us; it is a source of resentment that turns out to have very practical implications. For example, it has had a detrimental influence on the funding of economic research by the European Commission.

With respect to policy advice and social attitudes, economists often show what might be called the inherent conservatism of economics. Our *déformation professionnelle* is very much to trust markets to exploit the possibilities for Pareto-superior moves. To the extent that reality does approximate that view of the world, that is, insofar as people behave that way and that institutions facilitate the working of markets, what is left are trade-offs and possible policy moves in which there are going to be some losers. Typically the losers arc less diffuse, better organized and more vocal than the gainers. They will then block interventions, so there will be an underlying conservatism in the way in which policy recommendations work out.

Forecasting

We are often tarred by the brush of failed forecasts. The problem is that failure in economic forecasting is highly visible. It is brought out on the television. It hurts our public image and, indeed, to a significant extent the economic profession is identified with forecasting, whereas in fact we know that most economics is not like that. Most of our work, however, will not get us in the media.

There are many phenomena that we simply do not understand very well: what we know is how little we know. For example, there has been an immense amount of empirical research on the short and medium run behaviour of exchange rates, but this remains one of those problems that simply is very difficult to solve. Likewise we do not fully understand labour supply and labour demand and their interaction: there is a considerable disagreement in the journals about the effects of a minimum wage or whether the NAIRU has fallen in the United States. We do not know the answers yet, so we cannot forecast well in these important areas.

The combination of perceived irrelevance, apparent disagreement and failures in forecasting has led to scepticism about the ability of the professional economics community to choose the best research and the best researchers. There are doubts about the validity of peer review itself and the extent to which it may reinforce mainstream orthodoxy. It is argued that peer-group processes may be self-perpetuating; in the limit, it is suggested that these processes may corrupt (if not explicitly, then implicitly). Sceptics argue that peer-group reviewing ignores broader criteria.

3.2 Proposed Remedies

Will we be able to match demand (that is, research issues that interest users) and supply (that is, high quality research)? What are the solutions that our critics propose? Two remedies have been suggested by the research funding community:

- answer the questions set by 'users'; and
- do more 'priority-directed' research - and let funders 'pick winners'

Users
We are told that the users of economic research have to define the issues that we should be addressing and the research that should be funded. Consider, for example, the following quote from the preface of the 1995 *ESRC Business Directory*:

> The Economic and Social Research Council [ESRC] is the UK's leading research and training agency addressing economic and social concerns. We aim to provide high quality research on issues of importance to business, the public sector and government. [We are committed] to funding high quality research that meets the needs of its consumers.

This is particularly worrying because the ESRC has in the past been the major funder of *basic* research in the social sciences in the United Kingdom.

Picking the winners
There is always pressure to draw public funding towards more broadly 'priority-directed research', that is, research that helps to pick the winning firm or the winning policy prescription. This pressure is exerted by the 'wealth creation culture' that demands concrete results. Researchers are asked to deliver in a way that tends

to bias the research activities towards a kind of short-termism which
is bad both in the intellectual sphere and in the 'markets' for socio-
economic analysis and policy prescription.

3.3   Why This Won't Work

This approach will not work for two fairly obvious reasons: user
priorities shift faster than researchers can deliver; and no one can
foresee either the questions of tomorrow (let alone next year) or the
applications of theoretical advances.

Users and their priorities
First, the priorities of users are very short-term themselves. Users
work in government departments and corporate staff departments, and
it is tough out there. The problems come across their desk very fast,
and they have to provide answers immediately. Today's problem is
forgotten tomorrow; and tomorrow's problem is not foreseen today,
simply because there is no time to reflect on what tomorrow's
problem is going to be.

More important, however, is the fundamental fact that the users
can simply not foresee now what will be the relevant questions given
the time horizon of a research programme. The gestation period of a
research project begins now. The user has to specify the research
rationale, set the priorities, get the resources, get the funding and
perhaps go out to tender. The funders have to select and commission
projects. The researchers have to hire staff, get the data, do the
research, write it up, and then disseminate it in a form that policy-
makers can understand. All that takes time. It is not sensible to think
that you can get answers to today's immediate problems by going out
and commissioning research projects.

The need for 'blue-sky research'
Moreover, as far as theory is concerned one can simply not foresee
the applications of theoretical research. DNA is an example. In 1950
a Ministry of the Interior would certainly not have been able or
willing to fund research on DNA, although this has ultimately
provided an extremely useful tool for identifying criminals. Research
on DNA was typical 'blue sky research'. It was not done with a

direct application in mind. Likewise much of what is going on in modern academic economics is blue sky research. And rightly so.

Europe and its individual nations need world-class, curiosity-driven, basic research. You cannot simply import this kind of knowledge; you cannot just read the American journals. A firm needs staff who can recognize and understand innovative research. Likewise in order to import economic knowledge and apply it effectively, a country needs a domestic research base. This should be a base of people who actually do work in the same way as the international research community, although they do not necessarily come up with the same range of results.

The conventional contrast between 'blue-sky', basic research and applied research is misleading. Blue-sky research contributes to problem-solving expertise. Research in this sense is directed towards simplifying complex behaviour. This is not done to make the research abstract, incomprehensible and irrelevant but rather to make it possible to deduce some generalizations that can then be applied to other different, but equally complex, data. Such research can then be applied to specific circumstances that cannot be foreseen now when the research is being initiated and done.

A related problem is that users want straightforward answers. Academic economists, however, find complexity in social behaviour, recognize the complexities and tend not to oversimplify the issues. So here economists are pointing out the pros and cons: 'on the one hand... on the other hand...'. One-handed economists are very scarce. But policy makers do not want questions, they want an answer.

Given the instability and unpredictability of user priorities and questions, I would suggest that it is more important for academic economists to provide the analytical framework and to elucidate the arguments rather than to get the answers to today's questions. The policy makers themselves had better get the answers. Academic economists can show policy makers how they can solve problems, but academic economists cannot start from the particular circumstances that the policy makers are going to face in any specific application in the future.

3.4   What Are the Real Problems?

Many of the points that we have been discussing so far are essentially
misperceptions and misunderstandings. These problems can be solved
- at least in principle - if academic economists improve
communication with the policy makers and the funders. They need
wider, better targeted, clearer and better expressed dissemination of
their work. Fairness compels me to admit that this is not a
comparative advantage of the academic economist. Indeed, academic
economists should be grateful for the 'gatekeepers' that work in
between the decision-makers and the academics: the specialized civil
servant or the good economic journalist or the corporate economist
who interprets the output and helps the decision-makers to recognize
good research and to apply academic work to current problems. We
should do our best to cooperate with the gatekeepers, because they
play a very important role. We should be concerned that their
numbers appear to be decreasing (in particular, in companies the
number of strategic planners and economists is being reduced
drastically).

Beyond all the misunderstanding and misperception, I see three key
real problems that create 'abuse' and that confront academic
economic life as a profession:

- how to stop users from intervening too far upstream in the
  research production process;
- how to get good research funded, given that economic research
  is by and large a public good, whereas users often desire
  privately appropriable results; and
- how to prevent capture, that is, the danger that the user will
  seek to influence the outcome, which is the greater, the more
  specific the 'use'.

I believe we do have a problem in preventing the abuse and misuse of
economic research by critics - and funders - who push academic
economists too far towards trying to be 'useful'. I am firmly
convinced that this is shortsighted and fundamentally misguided from
their point of view too.

Economics as a profession

I take comfort, however, in the fact that economics is a profession in the conventional sense of the term, exhibiting for example internally defined standards and self-regulation. Over centuries, in our own domain as well as many others, professions and professional criteria have been developed. These institutions have been able to meet a market test. The historical success of professions illustrates not only the robustness of monopoly power: society on balance *benefits* from professional groupings and from the standards and criteria that they impose. This is the fundamental objection to and defense against abuse by users. But we must use wisely and responsibly the privilege of being recognized as a profession.

4. Blood is Thicker than Water: Economists and the Tinbergen Legacy

Harry P. van Dalen and Arjo Klamer

European economists constitute a distinctive breed. At least so it seems when they are compared with American economists. They make the impression of being less academic than their American counterparts, more empirically and policy oriented, and less communicative and ambitious. Various studies have brought out the contrasts. A survey by Frey et al. (1984), for example, bears out the ideological differences with European economists much less convinced of the powers of market forces than the Americans. Not surprisingly, therefore, European economists play a much more significant role in public life than their American colleagues. Complaints about the crowding out of academic economists in the political arena - so common in the US (*cf.* Krugman 1994; Klamer and Meehan, 1994) - are rarely heard in Europe.

The Dutch economists appear to fit the European image. They have produced a remarkable number of prominent Dutch politicians and they take an active part in the numerous advisory councils that characterize Dutch politics. Yet nowhere in Europe do we observe the influence that one single economic research institute is having on policy, as that of the Central Planning Bureau (CPB) in the Netherlands. A brainchild of Tinbergen, the first Nobel prize winner for economics, the CPB is the official oracle of the Dutch government; whatever economic policy topic emerges, will not pass without the stamp of approval of the CPB. Such a stature for a group of serious economists would be inconceivable in the US and is not matched by any other group in Europe. This institution makes the Netherlands a special case, even in the European context.

The following story focuses on the Dutch. It will highlight the imprint of Tinbergen but it will try to answer the question that haunts everyone who is interested in the European quality of European economics: is European economics in the process of being Americanized? In an earlier study Klamer predicted that the observed differences between American and European economists will persist for the reason that they are a consequence of deeply rhetorical differences which, in turn, reflect different ways of thinking (Klamer 1995). Frey and Eichenberger (1993) foresee the Americanization of European economics and are not enthused. Many signs affirm their perspective (and fear). In the Netherlands the Americanization appears to have become the dominant trend in the world of economists since the early 1980s, when a noticeable number of economists who had received parts of their education in the US or the UK, returned to Holland, and graduate schools were set up modeled according to Anglo-Saxon style. Around the same time rankings of economists and economic programs began to appear and the pressure on publication was on. The rhetoric seemed to be changing from 'getting on and doing one's job' to 'getting international publications and going to the US for conferences'. International reputation is increasingly getting important for Dutch academic economists.

Does this international focusing of academic economics in the Netherlands pay off? Those who bear a warm heart towards the Dutch case will point out that the Dutch econometricians are of world class quality: the University of Amsterdam, the Free University and the Erasmus University are ranked 16, 28 and 44, respectively on a worldwide ranking of research activity in econometrics for the period 1980-1988 (see Hall, 1990). Admittedly, these numbers are not bad, but they are not very good either given the specialized econometrics programs at Dutch universities which allow students to concentrate on econometrics right after high school. Furthermore, the advanced econometric practice does not appear to have spill-overs to economic theory. At the moment Dutch academia is, putting it bluntly, backward. As the recent research assessment report of the Barten committee points out there are only a few excellent research groups in the Netherlands, notably CentER (van Damme and Tijs, game theory), Free University (Nijkamp, regional economics), Erasmus

University (Kloek, econometrics), and the University of Amsterdam (Boot, financial economics, and van der Ploeg, macroeconomics). The majority of the programs are indistinctive, certainly if placed in an international context.[1] Most research was evaluated as 'highly competent, admirably solid, but not truly venturesome' (VSNU 1995, p. 10).

This measured backwardness intrigues. The obvious question to ask is what prevents the Dutch from reclaiming the international stature that they once had with economists like Tinbergen, Theil and Koopmans? Is it a matter of time? At the end we will venture an answer, but, we hasten to add, the answer remains tentative. We are on more secure ground when it comes to characterizing Dutch economists *vis-à-vis* American economists. The reason is that our characterizations are drawn from a survey and discussions with a wide variety of economists.

The chronological order of the paper reflects our thoughts and prejudices during the process of collecting questionnaires and interviewing economists. First of all, we will start with the simple question which sparked off this research in the first place: Are the Dutch economists different from foreign economists, the American economists in particular? We were especially curious to find out whether the new graduate students were 'Americanized' in their American styled programs. If so, their responses to our questions should match the responses that American students gave in Klamer and Colander (1990). At any rate, our hypothesis was that a generation gap has come about in Dutch economics with the young Dutch economists much more mathematically-minded, less policy oriented, less quantitative, and more academically focused. If so, the Americanization of Dutch economics would be a fact.

The first results of the survey were disappointing. No clear patterns jumped out, nothing like the startling contrasts among schools that the American questionnaire had exposed. The tables presented a boring picture with a consistent grouping around the middle. What to make of this, we wondered? The numbers were not telling a story, at least not an interesting one.

The questionnaire provided us with an important clue, though, and this was the eminence of Tinbergen in the world of Dutch economists. He is without question the economist that Dutch economists respect most. This clue became our lead in the subsequent series of discussions with Dutch economists. (Klamer and Colander, 1990, used the same mixture of surveying and interviewing in their study.) The interviews confirmed the eminent stature of Tinbergen in Dutch economics but also showed that his impact is waning among the new generation. They compelled us to reinterpret some of the findings of the survey. Questions emerged about the consistency between what Dutch economists preach and what they practice. Might it be that Dutch are less policy-oriented than they claim to be, and that their research is less relevant than they want it to be?

4.1 Is the Dutch Economist Really Different?

Economists, be they European or American, are trained in macroeconomics and microeconomics with similar techniques and similar textbooks. One would not expect, therefore, that they come up with different answers to one and the same question. Still somewhere along the line, Europeans seem to differ from Americans in that they attach different weights to different tools, authorities and institutions. Table 4.1 gives us a nice impression of how different the Dutch economist is compared to economists elsewhere in the world.

The Dutch are, just like other Europeans, not outspoken. If the Dutch economist would utter his famous last words they would certainly be 'Ja, maar...' (Yes, but...). Americans and Canadians are less distracted by the nuances of a complex world: they more readily occupy radical positions supporting floating exchange rates and blaming minimum wages and trade unions without buts and ifs.

How can one understand these differences? Are European economists trained differently, are they more impressed by the history and culture of their country than Americans or are the intrinsic incentives different across countries? For a long time, one could earn an agreeable living as an economics professor in Holland by acting or being the policy adviser. Full professors were not pushed to publish and some did not even experience the hardships of writing a dissertation. The academic professional, the dominant character inside American academia, hardly earns a living in Holland, for one thing because the Netherlands, despite the efforts of the Dutch to reclaim land from water, remains a small country.

Table 4.1   Economic opinions across countries

	US	Can	NL	UK	Fra	Swi	Ger	Aus
Sample (*n*)	464	443	627	981	162	199	273	91
A minimum wage increases unemployment among the young and unskilled								
Agree	57	68	41	20	17	36	44	30
Agree with provisions	22	17	34	49	21	25	25	34
Disagree	21	15	22	21	60	30	30	35
No clear opinion	1	0	3	10	3	10	1	1
Tariffs and import quotas reduce general economic welfare								
Agree	71	70	53	25	27	47	70	44
Agree with provisions	21	26	36	49	44	40	24	42
Disagree	7	4	7	13	27	10	6	13
No clear opinion	1	0	4	12	3	3	1	1
Inflation is primarily a monetary phenomenon								
Agree	40	43	19	10	11	31	25	13
Agree with provisions	30	32	32	32	19	35	31	28
Disagree	29	24	39	41	68	33	43	56
No clear opinion	1	0	10	17	3	1	2	3
Wage-price controls should be used to control inflation								
Agree	8	5	13	5	25	9	2	18
Agree with provisions	18	21	40	28	29	30	5	30
Disagree	74	73	38	42	43	61	92	52
No clear opinion	0	0	10	14	3	0	1	1
The economic power of labour unions should be significantly curtailed								
Agree	-	26	9	-	19	19	21	18
Agree with provisions	-	33	32	-	22	28	35	29
Disagree	-	38	56	-	54	51	44	53
No clear opinion	-	3	3	-	4	2	1	1
Antitrust laws should be enforced vigorously to reduce monopoly power								
Agree	35	33	46	24	56	37	55	49
Agree with provisions	30	38	43	40	37	45	34	36
Disagree	29	27	29	15	6	19	10	11
No clear opinion	6	1	3	21	1	0	1	3
'Consumer protection' laws generally reduce economic efficiency								
Agree	18	14	6	4	5	18	10	7
Agree with provisions	24	31	22	14	17	26	24	22
Disagree	56	52	67	50	77	56	65	70
No clear opinion	2	3	6	21	1	1	1	1
Effluent taxes are a better to control pollution than imposition of pollution ceilings								
Agree	56	49	40	19	27	21	34	21
Agree with provisions	23	32	30	40	27	34	30	22
Disagree	21	17	19	25	41	43	33	55
No clear opinion	1	2	11	16	5	2	3	2
The welfare system should be restructured along lines of a 'negative income tax'								
Agree	44	52	19	23	18	19	21	22
Agree with provisions	34	35	27	46	33	25	26	28
Disagree	19	11	38	15	43	54	46	43
No clear opinion	3	2	16	16	6	3	7	8

Source   The figures for foreign countries are taken from US: Alston et al. (1992); Canada: Block and Walker (1988); UK: Ricketts and Shoesmith (1990, 1992); France, Switzerland, Germany and Austria: Frey et al. (1984).

The roles Dutch economists take on in discussing their work and convincing their audiences is at the focus of our attention. However, the starting point for our discussion is not Dutch but American. Dutch academia is starting to change to an American style of practicing economics and if one wants to understand the Dutch economists of the present day one should start taking a closer look at what is happening across the Atlantic.

Table 4.2   Perceptions of success

	Dutch graduates	Dutch PhDs 'new style'	US graduates
Being smart and good at mathematical problem solving			
Very important	56	66	65 '
Moderately important	34	30	32
Unimportant	8	4	3
Don't know	2	0	1
Interested in, and good at, empirical research			
Very important	52	36	16
Moderately important	38	58	60
Unimportant	7	6	23
Don't know	3	0	1
Being very knowledgable about one particular field			
Very important	33	48	37
Moderately important	53	38	42
Unimportant	12	14	19
Don't know	3	0	2
Ability to make connections with prominent professors, networking			
Very important	40	56	26
Moderately important	44	36	50
Unimportant	10	6	16
Don't know	6	2	9
Having a broad knowledge of the economics literature			
Very important	48	8	10
Moderately important	35	56	41
Unimportant	14	36	43
Don't know	3	0	5
Having a thorough knowledge of the economy			
Very important	38	12	3
Moderately important	40	46	22
Unimportant	16	40	68
Don't know	7	2	7

In touch with the real world

One of the striking findings in Klamer and Colander's *Making of An Economist* (1990) which triggered the awareness of the economics profession that something was wrong with graduate education and the profession in general was the response of US graduates to the question 'Which characteristics will place graduate students on the fast track?' Puzzle solving and mathematical skills came on top and empirical skills and knowledge of the economy on the bottom (reproduced in Table 4.2). This finding came as a shock to most economists and it provoked a discussion of what's wrong with American graduate training and more or less induced the American Economic Association to establish the Commission on Graduate Education in Economics (Hansen, 1991).

To see how different Dutch economists are from their American counterparts we posed this and many other questions in a survey that we sent between May and September 1995 to approximately 1,500 economists (264 graduates, 102 former graduates, 105 professors of economics and a random selection of 1,000 members of the Royal Dutch Economic Association).[2] The overall response rate was 43 per cent, which is a satisfactory statistic for this type and length of questionnaire. We found that the answers of the Dutch graduates differ substantially from the American survey. Although the majority of the Dutch graduates (so-called 'AIOs') agree that puzzle-solving skills are very important (56 per cent versus 65 per cent of the Americans), empirical research ranks much higher in their assessment. Like in the American survey 'thorough knowledge of the economy' is ranked lowest but contrary to the Americans the Dutch give no reason for journalists to rush to the presses with the message that Dutch economists do not care for economic reality; whereas 68 per cent of the Americans considered this knowledge unimportant for success in the economics profession, only 16 per cent of the Dutch graduates think so. The great majority of the Dutch consider knowledge of the economy at least somewhat important to make it as an economist. Their answers confirm the Dutch preference for empirical research.

This is not to say that the American students in the Klamer–Colander study disparaged empirical research altogether as the journalist accounts suggested. Especially in conversation the American students revealed their frustrations with the situation. They perceived the low value attached to 'thorough knowledge of the economy' but most of them cared about such knowledge themselves. The few Chicago students who proudly announced that they did not care about reality, were the exceptions. Overall the American graduates turned out to be frustrated with the emphasis on techniques and mathematics in the profession and would like to see it differently. Chicago students made jokes about professors with mainly technical and mathematical interests (Klamer and Colander 1990, p. 148); MIT students complained about the technical nature of the papers that got presented in seminars (Klamer and Colander 1990, p. 82). What emerged from these conversations was appreciation for professors who apply their economics to the real world and policy issues. Accordingly, what they valued in economics conflicted with what they perceived to be the ruling values.

The main difference between them and the Dutch students is then that the latter do not sense a conflict. Surely, we got complaints about the mathematical direction that the discipline is taking but nobody in particular seems as frustrated as the Americans are. The technical nature of the discipline does not overwhelm the Dutch graduates. They share the American appreciation for clever, applied work that gives insight in the real world and we find similar heroes in people like Krugman.[3] If the Dutch were to experience a conflict between what they value in economics and what they perceive to be the reigning values, the conflict is minor.

On diversity

The Dutch economists, the graduates included, are much less diverse than their American counterparts. They do not go in schools as the Americans do. The existence of distinct schools was one of the major findings of the Klamer-Colander study. Chicago economists are different from MIT economists, and MIT economists are different from Harvard economists (even though they operate at one mile's distance from each other). The differences showed in the responses of their students to questions about economics and to economic propositions. When zero per cent of the MIT students disagree with the proposition that fiscal policy can be an effective stabilizer versus 44 per cent of the Chicago students, there is a difference. And what to say of a zero versus a 41 per cent contrast in their agreement with the constant money growth rule? (You may guess which school produced the zero.) Harvard students proved to be much more sceptical of the justice of the market mechanism than any other group of students.

The survey among the Dutch economists produced no such diversity. The sample manifests a significant dose of scepticism towards the ruling paradigms in economics but we were unable to detect distinctive schools of thought, that is, economists who go in groups and are eager to distinguish themselves from other groups. In Chicago students will sneer at ideas of MIT economists, such as the efficiency wage hypothesis and Harvard students will snigger when names of outspoken Chicago economists come up. Lively and intense gossip serves to maintain the sense of distinction and of being part of a school. At Chicago students get to hear from Lucas that they do economics differently, seriously that is, with the implication that elsewhere economics is done too much to please policy makers. Dutch economists do not take such outspoken positions and if they do, they do so as individuals.

The absence of schools of thought in Dutch economics agrees with the pragmatic and anti-ideological approach of Tinbergen. It shows in the resistance of Dutch economists against any labeling. They prefer to be considered eclectic and they see themselves as neutral experts. It is tempting to attribute this aversion to labels and schools to the Dutch partiality towards consensus. A counterinstance would be the existence of schools in sociology, with a dedicated group of followers of Elias as an especially distinctive school of thought. Puzzling might also be the separation of econometricians in a distinctive group although they distinguish themselves in their scientific interests, not in their economic and ideological opinions. At any rate, these two anomalies do not justify the rejection of the thesis that a pragmatic and anti-ideological stance deters the formation of schools in Dutch economics.

The pain of socialization

Where schools exist, socialization processes occur. Students need to be initiated into the ways of thinking that characterize a particular school. To American students the choice of graduate school has strong consequences especially when it is a school like Chicago, University of Massachusetts, George Mason University, or any other school with a distinctive program. In the Netherlands, the choice of graduate school does not matter much, partly because the schools collaborate. And without distinctive schools to join or to keep their distance from, the Dutch students do not perceive themselves getting socialized. Where American students talk about getting brainwashed and about changing their mind on important issues under influence of their schools, the Dutch students shrug their shoulders. They may be critical and sceptical at times, but they do not feel pressured to change their perspective. In general, they appear to be pleased with their experiences in graduate school, much more so than the American students.

If anything is in doubt it is their commitment to the science of economics. Their frustrations notwithstanding, 73 per cent of the American graduates would choose to do graduate studies in economics again. The Dutch students are less sure; of them 64 per cent would do it again. One reason for the difference may be the bleak prospects that the academic market offers the Dutch students. When asked what they would like to do after graduate school, only 37 per cent aspires to be an academic scholar. The next most desired career is that of a researcher (28 per cent). A government job, the most likely outcome, scores only 8 per cent as the career desired most by the Dutch graduate students. American graduates are definitely more committed to academia.

Another way to detect how 'American' the economics profession has become is to look at who or which institution is influential. When we took our (Dutch) classes in economics there was only one view of what makes the economy tick and that view was the one brought forward by the CPB. This was the impression one could get some ten years ago if one listened to the Dutch discourse in economics. Debates about economics were usually debates about the opinions and declarations of the CPB.

With the appearance of graduate schools things have become different. These schools lured back Dutch economists who were working abroad (primarily in the US and the UK). They furthermore invited prominent foreign economists, mainly from the US, to give graduate seminars. With the rise of status of academic economics, the reputation of the CPB among economists began to fade (see Table 4.3). Whereas older economists still rank CPB as having most influence on their thinking, young economists have little attention for the CPB. Revealing is the choice of heroes. Dutch graduate students of today like especially Krugman ('is good at everything'), Arrow ('Almost everything is in Walras, the rest is in Arrow'), Lucas and Romer. The majority of the respected economists is American.

Table 4.3   Authorities in Dutch economics

	Average economist	Graduates	Young < 40 years	Middle aged 40-60	Old ≥ 60 years
1. Academic economist					
Very important	33	39	36	28	34
Moderately important	53	51	52	57	51
Hardly important	12	8	10	14	12
Unimportant	1	1	2	1	3
2. Foreign institutions (like IMF and OECD)					
Very important	26	18	21	33	32
Moderately important	55	56	57	51	55
Hardly important	17	24	19	15	11
Unimportant	2	2	3	1	2
3. Central Planning Bureau					
Very important	24	4	14	32	43
Moderately important	51	50	51	52	51
Hardly important	20	34	28	13	4
Unimportant	5	12	8	3	1
4. Staff departments at ministries					
Very important	7	2	5	11	9
Moderately important	42	39	41	44	39
Hardly important	42	49	45	37	46
Unimportant	9	10	9	8	6
5. Business consultancy firms (McKinsey, KPMG)					
Very important	8	6	6	9	10
Moderately important	33	29	31	34	40
Hardly important	43	42	43	43	40
Unimportant	17	22	20	14	10
6. Parliamentary spokesman					
Very important	2	1	2	2	2
Moderately important	17	21	18	14	20
Hardly important	58	52	56	61	58
Unimportant	24	26	25	24	20

The fading of the CPB is easy to understand. If Dutch economists want to succeed academically, they have to be on the frontier of economic science and large-scale modelling, the preoccupation of CPB economists, is no longer considered science among economists. Large-scale modelling is necessary and perhaps considered useful by insiders, but it isn't science. Van Wijnbergen aired his grievances about the CPB during our interviews:

> They give answers based on models which no one really seems to understand. We only know that these models give the wrong answers to big shocks and for small shocks they are not relevant. The Planning Bureau has a model which is used for all kinds of problems. This is a big mistake. They cannot take into account the behavioral reactions of people in case of fundamental changes or policy shifts. This is where the Lucas critique becomes important. (van Dalen and Klamer 1996a, pp. 109-10)

In the meantime the economists of the CPB are working towards an improvement in their academic standing without losing their standing in the policy world. It is not an easy task and the question is whether it can be done. One researcher told us about the difficulties he encountered in using an endogenous growth model:

> It costed us a lot of time and trouble to get this model [the Grossman-Helpman model] going, to calibrate it for OECD-figures, but in the end numbers appeared. To our disappointment this simulation exercise did not contain anything new for academic economists and at the same time we were told by the board of the Planning Bureau: 'Well, it is rather abstract'. The results were not entirely crazy and the only policy advice you can distill from these types of models is that it would be wise to invest in education. Well, there's policy relevancy for you!

Another CPB researcher takes a more pragmatic view:

> I look upon us as users of economic science. If economic science takes a different turn we try to jump on the bandwagon and use it for our purposes, if it fills our needs. Because of this strategy you're not at the frontier of science. You don't want to run along with every new development in economics because sometimes those bubbles burst. We simply are users and that's why we have less to offer to economic science. (van Dalen and Klamer 1996a, p. 189)

Pragmatism also dominates the methodological positioning of Dutch economists. Whereas most American graduates would support the thesis that 'Economics is the queen of the social sciences', the majority of Dutch graduates disavow this claim. Their scientific modesty might be at least a partial explanation of the limited visibility of Dutch economists in the international arena. As Stigler (1955, p. 5) once put it:

> New ideas are even harder to sell than new products. One must put on the best face possible, and much is possible. Wares must be shouted - the human mind is not a divining rod that quivers over truth. The techniques of persuasion also in the realm of ideas are generally repetition, inflated claims, and disproportionate emphases, and they have preceded and accompanied the adoption on a large scale of almost every new idea in economic theory.

Table 4.4   Opinions of economics as a science

	Dutch graduates	Dutch PhDs 'new style'	Dutch MAs	Chicago	MIT	Harvard	American graduates
Neoclassical economics is relevant for the economic problems of today							
Strongly agree	38	48	55	69	31	20	34
Agree somewhat	38	30	37	28	56	56	54
Disagree	13	14	5	3	11	22	11
No clear vision	11	8	4	0	2	2	1
Economists agree on fundamental issues							
Strongly agree	8	12	10	3	4	2	4
Agree somewhat	12	24	34	47	31	27	40
Disagree	73	58	54	44	60	68	52
No clear vision	7	6	3	6	4	2	4
There is a sharp line between positive and normative economics							
Strongly agree	7	8	8	22	7	9	9
Agree somewhat	24	26	31	38	16	4	23
Disagree	49	44	38	34	73	84	62
No clear vision	20	22	24	6	4	2	6
Economics is the queen of the social sciences							
Strongly agree	11	12	21	47	27	9	28
Agree somewhat	18	14	27	28	36	43	39
Disagree	55	54	39	9	24	30	19
No clear vision	15	20	12	16	13	18	14

If one looks at these ingredients for academic success one can understand why the Dutch with their pragmatic and modest positioning have a hard time selling their products.

As Table 4.4 shows the majority of Dutch economists is sceptical of the possibility for agreement among economists. Chicago graduates are most outspoken in their belief that economists can reach agreement. Harvard and MIT students are more sceptical but still not as much as the Dutch.

4.3 Characters in Economics

The American students appeared to suffer from a case of mistaken identities. In conversation they revealed their desired identity as an economist, or at least what they had been looking for in a life as an economist before they entered graduate school, and told how that identity did not match the character that they learned to become in graduate school. Quite a few American graduates chose to study economics because they wanted to be an Intellectual in the sense that they expressed their desire to talk, explore, and to enter new territory - unbound by tradition and discipline - in pursuit of truth and interesting ideas. These students found to their chagrin that American graduate training stifles the intellectual with its emphasis on discipline in reasoning, on technique, and the strong discouragement of reading across disciplinary boundaries. Only at Chicago the intellectuals among the students felt encouraged. All the other schools failed to foster the intellectual values.

The next most important desired character was that of the Social Activist. The character manifests itself in declarations like 'I chose economics because I wanted to change the world', or 'I chose it to have influence on policy'. Heroes for the social activists are economists such as Keynes, Marx and Friedman. They are admired for their social concerns and their involvement as economists in worldly affairs. American graduate schools frustrate these characters as well. 'Those who can't do economics, do policy', is one of the slogans cited. People who were involved in policy were made fun of, or were subject to criticisms and doubts. Lester Thurow had the nickname 'Less than thorough'. The otherwise widely read work of Galbraith, a social activist *pur sang*, is virtually banned from the graduate curriculum. Even Friedman appeared to have lost his scientific stature at Chicago.[4]

Another important character for American students was the Teacher. Several indicated their desire to teach economics, because they found it important that people learn the insights of economics. Unfortunately for them, graduate school taught them that teaching is an activity to be avoided at all costs, for research is what the life of an economist is supposed to be all about.

Thus the American students learn to change the character that they expected to become. Instead of the intellectual, social activist, or teacher, they become in graduate school the Academic Professional, the celebrated character in academic life. Professionals they are supposed to be, because that is how they are socialized. Graduate schools screen those who want to be member of the profession and take each candidate through a series of rigorous tests. In the process students learn what professional behaviour is (for example, when a colleague asks for comments on a paper, give it to him or her). But unlike doctors and lawyers the economics profession is not set up with the intention to serve the public. The candidates quickly learn that the most important audience are academics themselves. They learn the tools of the trade not necessarily to advise and consult those outside the profession but to impress, entertain and intimidate fellow academicians with clever refinements and criticisms of the most advanced tools. When they perform to show off their skills, they do so in front of an academic audience without consideration of the lay audiences. The American graduate students indicated to be troubled by this imposed character of the academic professional. That is why Klamer and Colander (1990) speak of a case of mistaken identities.

Dutch economists do not share these confusions of desired and actual identities. They do not feel the pressure to conform to a specific character. The reason might be that the academic professional still is not the dominant character in Dutch academia. This may change, though. Notably, the program at Tilburg university impresses on its graduates the importance of operating in the international community; it follows the American approach with many foreign visitors coming through and a large variety of weekly seminars. Several AIOs expressed a desire to participate in the academic game, and consciously pursue the status of academic professional. The Dutch students who do not want to jump on the American bandwagon, though, do not as yet experience the pressure of changing their desired character to that of the academic professional to the extent the American students do.

The Researcher

Dutch academic training appears to be less restraining, less selective than the American one. It leaves open more room to students to fill in their own character. As a consequence the characters that make up the Dutch world of economists differ from the ones that Klamer and Colander encountered in the US. One of these is that of the researcher. This is the economist who does economics for the sake of research. He is not an academic professional because he lacks the commitment of the latter to the academic game; he most likely prefers to work at a research institute rather than a university. As a researcher he is less interested in advancing (academic) knowledge and techniques than in applying existing knowledge and techniques to real world problems. If compromises are needed to get results, the researcher is willing to go where the academic purist would refuse to tread. It is no surprise therefore that the researcher prefers to share his research with fellow researchers rather than with academic professionals. His objective is to do research that is relevant for decision making in policy and, possibly, business but as a researcher he is reluctant to 'sell' his findings to the possible users. That task he prefers to leave to others.[5]

The economists working for the CPB are the typical researchers. Insofar as we can speak of the CPB economist, he loves to do research, likes to be a scientist but he does not see himself to be quite up to speed, insists on the applicability of his research, is willing to make concessions when needed, and derives satisfaction from seeing the influence of his work on the policy process. The academic professional, in contrast, is foremost interested in the approval and appreciation of fellow academics. Researchers like to publish in academic journals, but an academic publication is no must for them; it *is* to an academic professional.

The character of the researcher continues to inspire Dutch economists: 28 per cent of the Dutch graduates professed their desire to be one.

The Policy Advisor

Another character that emerges in the Dutch conversations but failed to appear in the Klamer-Colander study is the policy advisor. This is the economist who seeks satisfaction and recognition as an economist in the policy arena. According to this character enlightenment of the policy process with the insights of scientific economics is what economics is all about. It is the character of Tinbergen and so many other Dutch economists who have participated, and continue to do so, in political processes in their quality as economics professor. Policy advisors are not the neutral technical experts as they are portrayed by the outside world but they also have their self-serving aims, namely, they want to get their advice accepted, no matter what. They will 'fight their corner' inside the government machine, so elegantly described by Heclo and Wildavsky (1974). And if that means that they have to make exaggerated claims or employ the Ricardian Vice, so be it. Policy advisors are in the persuasion business and their value stems primarily from getting their policy advice accepted in the fast lane in the Oval Office, No. 10 or the Dutch equivalent of these offices, 'het Torentje'. To put this in the civil servants' lingo: they want to set the political agenda.

This character exists in the US too, of course. Just think of the long line of respected and reputable academic economists who worked on the Council of Economic Advisors and research departments of Federal Reserve Banks (especially the Fed in Minneapolis). In contradistinction to the Dutch political activist, the American one usually has to be on leave from academia to perform as one, and when he stays academic, risks his academic stature. Krugman (1994) characterizes economists who are willing to compromise the science of economics just to get the ear of the policy makers as 'policy entrepreneurs'. He does not hide his disdain for such a character. Dutch economists who venture into the policy arena are not free from suspicions on the part of their academic colleagues but it will be relatively easy to maintain their position in academic life.

4.4   The Tinbergen Legacy

The key to understanding the development of the Dutch characters is Table 4.5. Economists who value the work and attitude of one economist so highly cannot be but moved and affected by the values of that same economist. Tinbergen (1903-94) is the most respected economist in the Netherlands. This finding together with the motivations that Dutch economists give for their choice helps to unravel the character of the Dutch economist.[6] Dutch economists are generally respected for their ability to link economic theory with practice. This ability characterizes well-liked and well-known (at least among the Dutch) economists such as Pen, van der Ploeg, Bovenberg, Zijlstra and Bomhoff. More than anyone else, however, Tinbergen stands as a model for all these economists with his reputation for combining theoretical and practical skills.

Table 4.5   *Most respected economists (number of votes in*
             parentheses)

American graduates	Dutch graduates	Dutch economists (PhDs and MAs together)
J.M. Keynes (58)	J. Tinbergen (16)	J. Tinbergen (158)
K.J. Arrow (35)	J.M. Keynes (15)	J.M. Keynes (119)
P.A. Samuelson (26)	P. Krugman (12)	J.K. Galbraith (35)
K. Marx (23)	G.S. Becker (8)	J.A. Schumpeter (35)
A. Smith (18)	A. Smith (8)	A. Smith (34)

Source: Own survey, and Klamer and Colander (1990, p. 41).

Tinbergen started off as a Researcher in his work for the United Nations, was an academic with positions at universities in Amsterdam and in Rotterdam, and became active in the policy world as director of the CPB, and later in international development organizations. Especially important is his involvement with the CPB which, as we have seen, was instrumental in developing post-war Dutch economic thought. Arguably, the CPB is his most important legacy to the world of Dutch economists. The CPB influence on Dutch academia was for a long time strong due to personal connections: researchers who started their career at the CPB often moved to academia where they essentially taught CPB-economics, that is, large-scale Keynesian macroeconometric modeling. The econometric modeling critique by Lucas (1976) did not have a major effect on the CPB approach, but in hindsight we may see it as a beginning of the fading of the reputation of the CPB in the Dutch academic world.

To see how strong the example of Tinbergen still is, we investigated to what extent the beliefs of Dutch economists reflect the values and scientific principles of Tinbergen. Musing on his professional experiences, Tinbergen (1979, p. 357) gave the following guidelines for scientific work:

- we try to minimize dogmatism and subjectivity;
- we remain as close to empirical data as possible;
- we work in interdisciplinary teams; and last but not least
- we choose areas relevant to the most pressing problems.

In his policy involvements Tinbergen displayed a clear preference for pragmatic and rational consensus solutions, a preference that suited the role of the CPB and informs the proceedings of the numerous advisory boards that direct the policy process in the Netherlands (see Klamer, 1990).

Similar values and preferences showed up in conversations with CPB-researchers. They project themselves as the unbiased applied scientists in search of the truth; the same stance we found in discussions with the economists of the ministries and the Dutch Central Bank. As one CPB-researcher formulated it:

> I think we use models as a medium to process information from numerous sources and to make that information consistent. The ambition is not to produce an optimal forecast. One of our goals is to be useful for the political debate, which means that we have to use the assumptions used by policy makers, even though we sometimes think that they're not tenable.

The desire to solve problems based on a consensus is reflected in the survey by the answers which capture part of the Dutch corporatist setting. Dutch economists still value the use of wage-price controls and, contrary to what one would expect, do not think that the economic power of unions should be curtailed (see Table 4.1).

Furthermore, when asked about the cause of unemployment most economists pointed to the 'wedge' between gross and net wages and the unemployment trap (that is, small difference between net minimum wages and unemployment benefits). They do not consider one of the 'achievements' of consensus-economics, the uniformity of wage contracts across sectors of industry, responsible for the high Dutch unemployment rate.

Consistent with Tinbergen's beliefs, Dutch economists have a strong appreciation for empirical research. Among the total population of Dutch economists this skill ranked highest, to be followed by mathematical skills (see Table 4.2). US graduates do not value empirical research as high as the Dutch. The preference for empirical work is instilled in every Dutch economics student by their teachers, who refer to the work by the CPB and the scientific achievements made by Dutch econometricians like Theil, Cramer and Magnus (see van Dalen, 1997).

The desire to work in interdisciplinary teams sheds light on the puzzling statistic mentioned earlier: the Dutch do not think that economics is the Queen of the social sciences. In discussions with graduate students the desire to work in other scientific disciplines came up; the generally respected economists like van der Ploeg and Pen expressed the same desire.

Tinbergen's dedication to the socially most pressing problems like war and inequality is well known among the Dutch. He himself once motivated his interest as follows:

> I was interested in the problem of unemployment, the problem of poverty generally, and being a socialist and a member of the Socialist Party, I felt that I could be more useful as an economist than as a physicist ... My interest in economics was not primarily scientific, it was typically social. (Magnus and Morgan, 1987, pp. 118-19)

This social concern is endorsed by Dutch economists as reflected in their praise for Tinbergen: his social concern and the ability to link theory with practice. The older generation, however, is most outspoken in their endorsement.

Dutch economists carry on the leftist leanings of Tinbergen, who always has been a member of the Dutch socialist party (PvdA). Where one would expect strong support for free-market parties, 33

per cent of the Dutch economists voted for that same socialist party
(Table 4.6), whereas on a national scale only 24 per cent voted for
the socialist party. If we add to the number of votes allocated to more
or less left-wing parties such as the Green Left and the Democrats
D66 the median Dutch economist can be typified as left wing.

*Table 4.6   Voting behaviour of Dutch economists versus Dutch
citizens (per cent of votes)*

Party	Economists (total)	Graduates	National election
Labour party (PvdA)	33	32	24
Conservatives (VVD)	23	15	20
Democrats (D66)	19	24	16
Christian Democrats (CDA)	14	10	22
Green Left (Groen Links)	8	11	4
Other parties	4	8	15
Did not vote[a]	2	3	21

Note: [a] Per cent of the total of elegible voters.

4.5   Characters Causing Trouble in Paradise

Tinbergen and Frisch were the first economists to receive the Nobel
Prize in economics in 1969. With this landmark in the history of
economics the Dutch were perhaps lured into believing that they were
at the frontier of economic science and that policy-oriented work
could easily be combined with fundamental economic research. Dutch
economists have done plenty of important policy work but they have
failed to live up to the international role that they had imputed to
themselves. Wondering what has gone wrong we have to distinguish
between the research investments of the past and the present. It might
well be that things have been changed for the better but the effect of
those investments have not shown up in the appreciation of the
international scientific community.

 Still we would like to venture a number of stories that can explain
the present status of Dutch economics. To stay with the characters we

identify the key factors causing the backwardness with archetypes: (1) the social engineer; (2) the 'one-trick pony'; and (3) the economist who goes by the name of Stevenson's famous character: Dr Jekyll and Mr Hyde.

The social engineer

The character who lies at the heart of the backwardness of Dutch economics has a preference for 'useful' economics; a preference which is revealed by economists inside and outside academia. The Dutch economist likes to engineer economic solutions for society. Of course, anyone who values his own work will never claim that he or she is doing useless work. However, we would like to point out that usefulness in the present context refers to 'being of use to the policy maker'. Policy makers in The Hague are keen in knowing the economy-wide effects of every policy measure taken and the 'useful' economists are willing to be of service to the Mandarins by crunching numbers and mining data. The CPB has performed this role for decades and in their wake Dutch economists adopted its methodology and approach. In their 'scientific' endeavour they will use eclectic models; models in which economists blend theories of different persuasion in order to get a high R^2. Once this model has been constructed it is used again and again for every possible policy issue.

Of course, the term eclectic is an ambiguous term. Eminent economists like Solow and Samuelson would also call themselves 'eclectic' but they hardly fit the description of the useful economist. Eclectic in their vocabulary means approaching every problem with a different model. No model we know of can provide all the answers. It therefore stands to reason to be eclectic in the academic sense of the term. However, Dutch economics has for a long time been influenced by the way in which Tinbergen practised economic policy. The origins of the social engineer go back a long time in the history of Dutch economic thought. Throughout this history Dutch professors have been giving policy advice. They often held, besides their academic job, positions in government advisory committees (such as the Social and Cultural Planning Bureau, the Scientific Council for Government Policy and the Social Economic Council or the economically oriented ministerial departments). This is incidentally not just a post-war phenomenon, as is often believed in the

Netherlands, but has been the case ever since the liberal days of Vissering (1822-88), Mees (1813-84) and Pierson (1839-1909) (see Hasenberg-Butter, 1969). Accordingly, the professors formulated the demand for research in their role as economic policy advisor while at the same time in their role as a professor they could satisfy their earlier stated demands by supplying the necessary knowledge. Listen, for example, to the Tilburg economist Schouten, once a member of the Social Economic Council where academicians act as impartial third parties along with the unions and the employer organizations:

> If you don't have any contact with the Social Economic Council and if you only read the international literature, you don't come across this question [business cycles induced by a 'wage-push']. Because we were always talking about wage policies I wanted to know what happened if wages do not comply with the ideal norm. The theory is inspired by the Council. (Klamer 1990, p. 82)

Just to underscore the widespread influence of the CPB methodology we only have to mention that up to 1995 38 (!) of the body of economics professors have been employees of the CPB and most of them have been quite outspoken after they left the CPB. Generations of CPB economists and indeed also the 'old' Tinbergen (after 1945) tackled Dutch policy questions with just one method: large-scale macroeconometric models. Hypothesis testing which seemed to be the idea behind Tinbergen's earlier work on business cycles was no longer his leading motive, giving a plausible picture of the economy was his *leitmotiv* or as M.S. Morgan (1988) puts it 'finding a satisfactory empirical model'. The eclectic large-scale models themselves seemed to follow an evolutionary growth pattern where econometric and theoretic novelties were introduced with a sufficient time lag so as to minimize errors of being fashionable.

There are a number of reasons why economists living in the 'twilight zone' between economic science and economic policy do not make for good economics. The main reason is, of course, the claim by McCloskey (1996) that social engineering is impossible and illiberal. Social engineering simply does not work and those who think it does are fooling themselves. There are, however, still other reasons why social engineering has a bad influence on economic science. One of the major reasons was given years ago by the late Harry Johnson:

> People who go into government on a career basis become ... stale in their ideas, looking for ideas which really serve the Administration or what they think the Administration wants ... It is very difficult to resist the temptation to try to take credit for policy, and the pressures on the economist then are to try to shape his thinking so that he comes up with a policy which is saleable. [In addition,] they lose touch with the subject ... The people in government typically aren't all that good economists by the time they get somewhere. And what they're trying to persuade you is that bad economics is good politics and they are better at the politics, therefore, you should accept the bad economics. (cited in Allen, 1977, p. 61)

Of course, the danger of social engineers becoming a threat to economic science are smaller if academic economists are only temporarily involved in government policy making, as is the case with the Council of Economic Advisers in the US. The academic ties with influential government organisations in the Netherlands are generally on a permanent basis, thereby giving rise to the steady depreciation of academic human and social capital.

The one-trick pony

The second story can - in short - be described as 'choosing the wrong specialization' or 'running a lost race'. The economists populating the Dutch universities used to be academics who had mastered only one trick and this trick was exploited for the rest of their tenured lives. Sometimes this trick was handed down to the next generation of graduates. Minuscule schools of thought were formed that lived their lives in splendid isolation from developments in international science. The most outstanding examples of this type of research can be found in the work of Schouten, who built large-scale theoretical macroeconomic models with no behavioural underpinnings whatsoever, the large-scale macroeconometric model building by the CPB and its many epigones, or the Central Bank economist Kessler who told monetary stories with all kinds of elasticities. Dutch academia was dominated by academics huddled in the clothes of policy makers who furthermore were trained to master only one trick. It is therefore not surprising that foreign-trained economists do so well in the Netherlands. Being trained by Stone and other Cambridge economists like Meade, van der Ploeg gives an explanation of why, for instance, the English are in his opinion better economists:

> In Holland you are stuck with a research program and step by step you follow the plan stated in the program. You take a paper by a famous economist, you get six graduates to work on it, and that's it. I find that uninteresting, but the Dutch are quite good at it. The English, and I am in fact also one, are eclectic amateurs. This is, in my opinion, the most charming style around. Their motto is 'with a good pair of brains you can solve any problem'. (van Dalen and Klamer, 1996a, p. 123)

The real specialization within the Netherlands is still 'econometrics'. The specialization 'econometrics' was introduced into the Dutch economics education system in 1954 by Theil at the Erasmus University. However opportune such a specialization may have been at the time, with so many outstanding econometricians around, it has locked Dutch economics into a 'bad' equilibrium. The ideal of Tinbergen, to combine statistics with economic theory, has been lost.[7] Morgan (1990) concludes in her account of the history of econometrics that this applies in general to economic science, the most important consequence being the development of economics and econometrics as separate disciplines. Thanks to Theil the separation has been institutionalised in the Dutch educational system. Van Wijnbergen expressed his grievances most clearly:

> Tinbergen used tools and methods to solve economic problems. This is hampered by today's structure of the Dutch economic education. We have established an educational system in which people who have mastered the tools don't see the problems society is coping with, and those who do see the problems have no command over the tools. (van Dalen and Klamer 1996a, p. 110)

In the new graduate programs the division between economics and econometrics ceases to exist. Graduates are trained in macro-economics, microeconomics and econometrics. But, and this is where things go wrong, the undergraduate structure of the economics education is still a myriad of small departments where everybody seems to be doing his own type of economics. As shown in van Dalen (1997) about 80 per cent of Dutch economists produce their most important work on their own, whereas most American economists are more inclined to collaborate. A study by Smart and Waldfogel (1996) reports that 55 per cent of economists publishing in top journals produced their work on their own.

Table 4.7   Does econometrics breed indifference?

	Graduates with an:		
	Economics background	Econometrics background	Dutch Economists (total)
Inflation is primarily a monetary phenomenon			
Agree	24	16	19
Agree with provisions	29	25	32
Disagree	35	29	39
No clear opinion	11	31	10
Wage-price controls should be used to control inflation			
Agree	15	10	13
Agree with provisions	40	41	40
Disagree	35	18	38
No clear opinion	10	31	10
Flexible, floating currencies are an effective international monetary arrangement			
Agree	10	20	18
Agree with provisions	34	18	40
Disagree	35	25	30
No clear opinion	20	37	13
Rapidly and totally reforming a CPE is better than a slow and partial transition[a]			
Agree	24	10	19
Agree with provisions	18	12	20
Disagree	51	49	49
No clear opinion	8	29	11
The welfare system should be reformed along the lines of a 'negative income tax'			
Agree	17	8	19
Agree with provisions	29	19	27
Disagree	28	29	38
No clear opinion	27	44	16

Note: [a] CPE stands for Centrally Planned Economy

We found that the Dutch econometricians have less explicit views than the Dutch economists. Some do not see themselves as economists and when asked which economist they respected most

they could not think of one and some even apologized: 'I'm sorry.
I'm an econometrician, don't know any economics.' Econometricians
seem to be looking for yet another fine data-set which can fill the
needs of their newly designed test-statistic and they are not looking
for some problem to solve with their sophisticated box of tools. The
ignorance or indifference we came across might best be illustrated by
Table 4.7: econometricians are more inclined to have no opinion on
current economic problems or phenomena than economists.

The current developments in Dutch academia present us with an
interesting experiment because a second historical event is in the
making, namely, the reverse brain-drain of talent from abroad;
economists who do not have any firm intellectual roots in the
Netherlands. Whether the reverse brain-drain is a chance event is still
a matter of debate.[8] Some ascribe the reversal to the appearance of
'centers of excellence' and formal graduate schools, others are down-
to-earth and point out that 'American' Dutchmen are homesick, while
others (Tabellini, 1995) claim that Europe is an interesting place to
be with the construction of one European central bank and the
integration of economies. In other European countries the reversal of
the brain-drain is also becoming visible (for example, economists like
Laffont, Tirole and Tabellini have returned home).

Dr Jekyll and Mr Hyde

The concern for dogmas in economic policy debates and economics in
general resounded in almost every conversation we had with
economists inside and outside academia. Economists inside the
Treasury and the Ministry of Economic Affairs were worried about
the scientific level of economic discussions in the Netherlands.
Academics were considered too 'academic' and academic economists
and CPB economists were abhorred by the crudeness of arguments
and the dogmatism inside the government machine. The Dutch
economist's stated preferences come close to the scientific guidelines
Tinbergen (1979) once gave and which we summarized earlier.
However, the writings and behaviour reveal different preferences. In
short, the Dutch economist does not practice what he preaches. For
instance, given the moderate answers to most economic propositions
one would not expect dogmas or political ideology to play a role.
Still, thirteen of the fifteen propositions (normative and positive)

which we asked Dutch economists concerning economics are affected significantly (in a statistical sense) by the political ideology of the individual economist (van Dalen and Klamer, 1996b). Party ideology becomes especially significant in the everyday meaning of the phrase when economists have to state their opinion about 'hot' policy topics like the causes or cures of the Dutch unemployment problem and the ambiguous effects of the minimum wage.

So here we are with a picture of an ambiguous and uncertain economist: he wants to combine economic theory with practice or empirical research but he sticks to his specialization or research program; he thinks that ideology should not matter in economics and still it does matter; he appreciates in the true spirit of Tinbergen the contributions other disciplines make to economics, still he remains within the walls of his subject. And judging from the many research assessments the Dutch economists want to conquer the world and according to the Dutch minister of Education and Science we should aim at winning the Nobel Prize, but the Dutch economist does not take the pains to sell his product. Tinbergen never made exaggerated claims about his models and findings so why should he advertise his ideas. One can hear the economist think, 'The numbers tell the whole story and the policy makers can do as they choose with my findings. I am off to my next case'. However, times are changing and the style of research is becoming more American and less Dutch and as in all periods of transition the Dutch economist is in search of an identity, especially one which he or she can live up to.

4.6 Conclusions

The Dutch economists might make a special case. The dominance of one father figure, Tinbergen, is remarkable indeed. And so is the pivotal role that Dutch economists play in Dutch policy through one institution, the CPB. Unsurprisingly, that the latter institution also happens to be the brainchild of Tinbergen. Yet, with their policy orientation, their pragmatic approach to economics as a science, and their reservations about markets Dutch economists fit the image of the European economist as characterised by Frey and Eichenberger (1993).

So what can the Dutch story tell us about European economists? As we had thought before when we conducted our survey and conversations, Dutch economists are getting eager to run along with the developments in economic science across the Atlantic. The interest of the upcoming generation is turning away from policy and towards the academic game of publishing in the good journals and attending the right conferences. However, important differences remain, giving Klamer reasons to hold on to his thesis that rhetorical and cultural differences continue to differentiate American and European economists (Klamer, 1995). For one, the academic professional does not dominate the world of Dutch (European) economists as he does in the US. Whereas ambitious American graduates aspire the academic life, many Dutch hold out for policy and research-oriented work, guaranteeing the continuance of the policy advisor and the reseacher as the dominant characters in their world. (A reminder: the typical researcher works for a research institute and is not so much interested in academic recognition but cares most about getting practical results even if that means sacrificing academic standards of rigour and theoretical sophistication.) A good reason for this, apart from tradition, is the small size of the Dutch academic market.

An important motivation for the Americanization of Dutch (European) economics is the ambition to get American attention to the work of European economists. Ever since the Second World War everything significant that happens in economics as a science, appears to happen at the American side of the Pacific. So just as European politicians set up the European Community to break the American hegemony, European economists are organizing themselves to break the hegemony of American economics. Their strategy is Japanese: imitate the Americans and beat them at their own game in the international markets. The strategy is somewhat successful - European economists, and with them the Dutch economists, appear to do better in the international academic game and are getting more attention from the American economists - but certainly for the Dutch the success is less than overwhelming. No single contemporary Dutch economist comes even close to the reputation that 'oldies' like Tinbergen, Polak, Koopmans, Houthakker and Theil had and still have.

The Dutch story reveals a few major ambiguities in the current ambitions of Dutch economists. They may help to account for the continuing modest position of Dutch academic economics, the efforts of, for example, CentER in Tilburg notwithstanding. One ambiguity is that the Dutch economists want to hold on to the example of Jan Tinbergen, in particular his insistence on policy relevance and pragmatism. They want to be useful as economists. As a consequence, Dutch economists do a lot of empirical work that is attuned to the current interests of Dutch politicians and that is not the type of work that plays well internationally. Policy advisors and researchers generally do not make outstanding scientists. Economists who are able to hold on to academic recognition while doing policy work are rare, yet they seem to stand as models for young Dutch economists. It makes for a juggling act which the Dutch economists seem to mess up.

A further characteristic is the eclecticism to which Dutch economists are prone. Whereas the Americanization implies the disciplining of scientific practice according to the norms and strategies of the dominant neoclassical paradigm, many Dutch economists continue to embrace eclectic strategies and beat on drums that are out of tune with the American ones. Post-Keynesian economics, which is all but dead in American academia, is still alive and well in Dutch academia; economists at the CPB and the Dutch Central Bank still work on large scale macroeconometric models even though such models are academically dead since the Lucas critique.

Connected with this characteristic of eclecticism is the continuance of the Dutch focus on econometrics. Dutch economists appear to want to hold on to the reputation that Tinbergen, Theil, Koopmans and Houthakker built up in econometrics; it is the reason for the institutionalization of econometrics as a separate discipline. Outstanding econometricians they are not anymore, though, and now the econometric specialization appears to stand in the way of the development of the scientific economics, at least many think so including the Dutch economists who returned after a stay abroad.

In our book on Dutch economists (1996a) we advised that Dutch economists apply a sound economic principle: comparative advantage. Instead of competing with American economists on their terms, Dutch economists might do better developing the type of economics in which they have by chance or by tradition a comparative advantage. Once that advantage was in econometrics. Now it may be in geographical and spatial economics, possibly in labour econometrics; the Dutch also have by chance a few excellent game theorists in their midst. Yet, given their rich tradition in policy work Dutch economists may do better pouring energy into this work even if that does not bring them immediate academic recognition. Likewise, they are positioned to be a major force in the history of economic thought and economic history. Admittedly, these are minor fields with dubious reputations at the present, but the Dutch happen to have not only a rich tradition in this respect but also a few prominent economic philosophers in their midst. By gambling on the participation in the American mainstream, they risk not only having third rate American programs (as many American universities have become after they tried to emulate the example of MIT and Chicago) but also losing the comparative advantage that they still have. The other comparative advantage for Dutch economists may be the particular characteristics of the Dutch economy, including its history. The Dutch Golden Age has proved to be a gold mine for interesting economic research as the historian Schama and the economic historian de Vries have shown. The corporatist setting of post-World War II Dutch economy might prove to be just as interesting a case. If only Dutch economists had the vision to see the possibilities for distinction right under their eyes, Dutch economics might not only remain a special case but also become an exemplary one.

Notes

This paper was part of a larger project of which the results have been published in Dutch (van Dalen and Klamer 1996a). We gratefully acknowledge comments by Deirdre McCloskey.

1. A comparable statistic for the UK of the University Funding Council (Taylor and Izadi, 1996) shows that 10 out of 60 economics institutions were considered excellent. The Dutch figure is rather bleak: 4 out of 92 economics programs are considered excellent.

2. The survey was held in May 1995. A six-page questionnaire was sent to 1,461 economists, consisting of 264 graduate students, 92 PhDs (new style), 105 professors in economics and 1,000 members of the Royal Dutch Economic Association. A reminder note was sent in July 1995. The response rate of the graduate students was 56 per cent ($n = 149$), which

like the overall response rate is above average response rates for this type of questionnaire.

3. At the time of the American survey the star of Krugman still has to rise but Summers, the name that often came up then, projects a similar image of an empirically and policy oriented economist. Dutch economists also have found their Dutch equivalent of Krugman, namely, van der Ploeg (described by one of the graduates as 'a mini-Krugman').

4. The mood may have changed since the American survey was done. Several outstanding young economists have sought the spotlights in the policy arena and thus may have changed the standards for American graduates. Examples are Summers, assistant secretary of the Treasury; Krugman, who has left an indelible imprint on the public discussion of international trade issues; and Stiglitz, chairman of the Council of Economic Advisors.

5. The absence of the researcher in the American study may be due to the limited sample of economists for that study. Even so, we found more readiness among Dutch graduate students to become researchers than Klamer and Colander detected among the American students.

6. We hasten to add that the dominance of one economist in a European country is not a unique phenomenon. The influence of Nobel Laureate Frisch (1895-1973) in Norway is remarkably similar to the influence of Tinbergen in the Netherlands. The situation in Norway was once described as an 'intimate cooperation between politicians and economic experts' (Bergh, 1981, p. 133). Although an entire generation of Norwegian economists were educated in the spirit of the models of Frisch, his policy involvement seems to have been less influential than that of Tinbergen, or as Bergh (1981, p. 150) notes: 'Frisch's contribution seldom went beyond the technical aspects of model building'.

7. One should add however that Tinbergen viewed abstract economic theory which had no direct relationship with economic policy as useless. An aversion to pure economic theory has always been present in the Netherlands.

8. See for this terminology Arthur (1989).

5. Economist as Advocates: The Art of Making a Case

Jules J.M. Theeuwes

According to McCloskey (1983) economists use rhetorical arguments to make a point or built a case. Mäki (1995) in a discussion of McCloskey's seminal contribution defines rhetoric as (p. 1303): 'the use of arguments to persuade one's audience in an honest conversation'. All the tools of rhetoric are used to establish an economic theory or proposition. McCloskey (1987) illustrates the use of rhetorical tools by classifying the list of arguments economists might use to show that 'the demand curve slopes down'.

- Introspection: What would I do if the price of chocolate goes up?
- Thought experiments: What would others do if the price of chocolate goes up?
- Uncontrolled cases: After the oil crises Western demand for crude oil went down.
- Authority: Alfred Marshall said so.
- Symmetry: If the supply curve slopes up, the demand curve must slope down.
- By definition: Through the budget restriction: if expenditure on other goods remains the same, one can buy less chocolate if the price goes up.
- Theoretical arguments: see any micro textbook.
- Statistical evidence: see any econometric textbook.
- Analogy: If the demand for chocolate slopes down, then the demand for sex, drugs and rock-and-roll must slope down too.

The use of a set of rhetorical arguments is not how economists see their official methodological approach. The official methodology of economics is still very much based on the positivistic method as advocated by Popper and made popular in economics by Friedman (1953). According to the official methodology of economics the arguments economists have to use to show that 'the demand curve slopes down' are strictly based on a handful of generally acceptable axioms on the preference ordering and choice behaviour from which can be derived testable hypotheses. These hypotheses are tested with price and quantity data and if the coefficient in the demand function is significantly negative then the hypothesis of falling demand curves is not rejected or falsified. The hypothesis is not exactly proven either, but a large amount of statistical tests with different data sets in different countries at different times with all of them statistically significant negative coefficients makes the hypothesis almost true. Research on the work floor is not done according to the rules of the official methodology. As has been argued before there are many problems with this official methodology both from the statistical and econometric side (see, for example, Leamer 1983) and from the theoretical side.[1] Solow - while warning that McCloskey is in great danger of 'Going Too Far' - nevertheless agrees that she is 'right to deflate the pompous methodology of economics as science' (quoted in Mäki (1995), p. 1300).

When participating in public policy discussions economists drop all pretence of adhering to the methodological rules of the Popperian falsification process. When defending a case close to their (political) heart such as minimum wages, free trade. privatization, a fixed exchange rate, and so on, economists use all tricks in the book of rhetoric. They do not need to be ashamed of this. Economic rhetoric is the art of persuasion in open discussion with all honest means possible.

There is no 'Truth'

Economic rhetoric shares with the Popperian approach that there is no Truth with a capital T. There will always be many sides to any debate. The rhetoric of economics implies that economic discovery does not proceed as a one-directional process but is rather a slow, erratic, social process of making a case, drawing a crowd and building consensus. The best that the brightest can achieve for their ideas is a consensus but never unanimity. Economists are like a herd of sheep wandering through uncharted mountains shepherded by many sheep dog. There is lots of drifting among the flock and lots of lost sheep. Yet the hope is kept alive that we are ultimately driven in the right direction. Through the process of public discourse, of arguing in open forums (journals, books, conferences, workshops) dishonesty is found out, false economic ideas are corrected, outmoded ideas updated and correct ideas sharpened.

There are no train schedules for young economists which allow them to chart their travels from point A to point B. If economics is rhetoric then its practitioners need to know about the art of economics. They will have to learn that it is not possible to deal with everything at once and that there are many ways to deal with the same problem. They also need to know that rhetoric does not lead to anarchy and that enough competition between rhetorical arguments works in similar ways as Adam Smith's 'invisible hand' to achieve the common good of progress in economic knowledge. To expand on this I will in the rest of this chapter discuss the following three kinds of arts:

- the art of choosing a corner;
- the art of making a case; and
- the art of being honest.

The art of choosing a corner
I will first of all argue that it is impossible to be universal in economic discussions, it is impossible to cover all the bases. This implies that when making a case you have to choose your angle: static or dynamic, partial or general, equilibrium or disequilibrium. The tools of rhetoric can provide guidance when choosing a corner in a discussion.

The art of making a case
As there is no economic truth with a capital T, there are also no hard universally valid economic policy advices to be given. There are usually at least two sides to each argument. Hence one can only make a case. This implies that economists play the same role in the public arena as lawyers do in the court room. There is nothing wrong with

two armed economists, like there is nothing wrong with lawyers in a legal case.

The art of being honest

All this of course puts economics on much shakier foundations than we would have had if we did possess the straight and narrow path to the Truth. But that does not mean that we cannot be collectively honest. I will argue that the quality and honesty of the economic argument can be generated by allowing for competition and openness in the public discussion. I will plead for the importance of replication in this respect.

5.1 The Art of Choosing a Corner

Suppose we want to study the effect of subsidizing child care on the economy. Ideally, we would like to have the most general model, a general equilibrium model with supply and demand effects on all markets, with households, firms and a government sector. We want this model to predict for n periods and allow for s states of the world. We want to take into account all the relevant market imperfections. We all know that this is impossible. This impossibility is best illustrated by the following caption under a cartoon by Steven Tucker. The cartoon depicts a scene on a bench in a park where the obviously failed PhD student tells another student:

> My PhD thesis was a pioneering attempt to create a new synthesis by constructing a new-classical over-lapping generations equilibrium business cycle model with Austrian roots which nevertheless contained Keynesian price rigidities, neutrality properties, involuntary unemployment, outsider power, decreasing returns to scale, irrational expectations and maximising agents operating in a world of fundamentalist uncertainty, repeatedly hit by endogenous technical progress. When the model generated neo-Marxian predictions I just flipped![2]

The general, all encompassing super model is impossible and hence every model will have to be partial. Even the so-called 'general equilibrium model' is partial because it still implies a particular choice for equilibrium against disequilibrium. And it implies a choice for a market-and-price-mechanism approach neglecting institutional constraints and transaction costs. So when making a case we have to look for the right level of abstraction, for the right corner to come out of.

How does one know the right corner? Let me illustrate this by looking at a recent contribution which develops an interesting insight into the workings of the labour market: the Beaudry and DiNardo's 1991 model of wage adjustment. According to Beaudry and DiNardo (1991), changes in unemployment lead to wage adjustment in the labour market. These wage adjustments (certainly the downward changes) hit mostly at new entrants. Incumbents do not suffer from bad times at all or not as much, but they always profit from good times. This implies that the wages of incumbent workers are determined by the best employment situation since they were hired by the present employer. Beaudry and DiNardo contrast their model with two other models: the neoclassical spot market in which wages for new entrants and incumbents are determined by contemporaneous unemployment and the contract model in which wages of both groups are determined by unemployment at time of hiring. It will come as no surprise that their own contract model works best. I find the Beaudry and DiNardo model intuitively very appealing.

In the age-old discussion of unemployment and wage adjustment Beaudry and DiNardo came with a surprising new approach. They choose the right corner. Their article is very convincing. Why? An article becomes convincing and hence interesting the more rhetorical points it scores. The story which Beaudry and DiNardo tell can be checked off against at least five rhetorical points.

- Introspection (look at your own career and wage path).
- Uncontrolled cases (the university labour markets clearly experienced this type of wage adjustments in the recent past, as new entrants had worse wage paths than incumbents ever had).
- Theoretical arguments (well developed in their article).
- Statistical evidence (they use two data sets - one aggregate, the other by industry - and with comparable results).
- Analogy (their model fits well the high wage-unemployment elasticity which is found elsewhere for new entrants - an

elasticity of 3.0 - as compared to an average elasticity for all workers with a value between 1.4-1.6).

To conclude: a good contribution to economic science, and hence an addition to our economic assets, is a contribution that presents itself from a corner that fits as many dimensions of rhetoric as possible. A good corner is a corner from which one can accumulate lots of points of rhetorical persuasion.

5.3   The Art of Making a Case

A week before Christmas 1994 Leo van der Geest, the editor of the Dutch economic weekly *Economisch Statistische Berichten*, phoned me. He needed an article in a hurry, an article about misunderstandings and misconceptions in economics. We agreed that I should write an article making the point that the Dutch labour market is more flexible than is often thought (Theeuwes 1995).

Sclerotic market
It seems a foregone conclusion that the Dutch labour market is rigid and sclerotic. It is often said that the Dutch labour market is characterized by slow adjustments and lack of flexibility. Unemployed and employed workers are said to be very immobile, not willing to move or change when the state of the economy requires so. Matching efficiency, measuring the ease of putting a vacancy and a job searcher together, worsens over time (van Ours 1991). Wages are said to be inflexible; there is certainly no downward movement. Government intervention or pressure to generate wage moderation in the economy has been a constant policy objective in the Dutch economy since the second world war (Hartog and Theeuwes 1993).

Also long term unemployed, a dominant proportion of total unemployment, do not exert any downward pressure on wages in the Phillipscurve (Graafland 1990). Long term unemployment is more than half of total unemployment and hence wage adjustment is left to a minority of the unemployed job searchers. Downward adjustment of wages is often achieved because high skilled job searchers find jobs at lower functional levels and hence crowd out the lower skilled (Teulings 1990).

The labour market is entangled in a web of legal restrictions and regulations on working hours, working conditions, employment security, dismissal protection and so on. Wages are set in collective agreements which are almost always extended legally to parties not included in the bargaining. In his public lecture the present Minister of Finance Zalm (1990) discusses the negative effects on the labour market of this legal monopoly situation. The many layered and generous Dutch welfare state weakens supply incentives in the labour market (Gelauff and Graafland 1994). The case has been made over and over again so much that the term 'sclerose' became more associated with the Dutch labour market than with the human body.

Challenged by van der Geest, I did my utmost to make the opposite case. I learned that one makes a case by selective choice of rhetorical tools: by presenting the supporting evidence (as a lawyer does), choosing the appropriate examples and arguments and by leaving out conflicting and damaging evidence. Let me illustrate this procedure by giving counterarguments to five characteristics of the sclerotic labour market.

Slow adjustment?

In order to counter the idea of a sluggish, unadaptive labour market I stressed the big changes that the labour market has gone through. I made the case that the Dutch labour market had absorbed lots of new supply since the end of the Second World War. There were 3.8 million persons working in 1950 and almost double that (6.6 million) in 1994. Female participation had more than doubled in the 30 years since 1960: from 17 to 31 per cent. Over the same period we shortened average working time drastically. In 1950 a full time worker worked on average 2,370 hours per year. In 1993 the same full time worker was on the job for only 1,740 hours per year.

Clearly this picture of an expandable and adaptable labour market would have been coloured much differently if I had stressed instead that the total number of hours worked had hardly changed at all since the early 1950s (de Vries 1995).

Immobility?

To my own surprise it turns out that the yearly level of labour mobility (that is the percentage of job changers) is 15 per cent, which is comparable to other OECD countries. Also the level of gross job creation and destruction in a given year is internationally comparable (see Hassink 1996). From this point of view there is nothing specially rigid in the Dutch labour market.

To counter this favourable mobility view of the Dutch labour market I could have stressed the very low levels of labour mobility of elderly workers (40 years and older) on the Dutch labour market and would have noted that they will soon be an increasingly large part of the labour force as the large baby boom cohort grows older. Moreover the negative effect of aging on labour mobility in the Netherlands does not play to the fullest extent because elderly workers leave the labour market in increasingly large numbers at younger and younger age.

Inflexibilities?

In my article I also stressed the increasing importance of flexible and temporary labour contracts (8.6 per cent to 10.4 per cent between 1989 and 1994). I stressed that the Netherlands are the European champion in temporary work. Temporary work or help agencies ('uitzendbureaus') are a booming business. Temporary work through help agencies amounted to 2.5 per cent of employment in 1995. Temporary work is usually procyclical but in recent years one can detect a structural increase in temporary work employment in the Netherlands. But why temporary work, why not more flexible dismissal procedures?

The Netherlands has the highest percentage of part-time workers in Europa and even in the OECD. In 1995 more than one third of the Dutch worked part-time (37 per cent). The European average is less than half of that (16 per cent). Most of the part-time workers are women. One forgets the price they pay in terms of career perspectives

I mentioned that half the work force works at irregular hours at some time (evening, night, and weekend work). Furthermore in recent collective wage agreements and in the public discussions a trend has started to introduce much more flexible work times: total time was fixed but the starting time and length of the working day became variable.

Inflexible wages?

An important indicator of labour market flexibility is wage flexibility. According to the law of supply and demand a price should decrease to reduce excess supply. Translated to the aggregate labour market the law of demand and supply implies that wages should react negatively to the rate of unemployment. It turns out that this holds also on the Dutch labour market and that the size of this wage reaction coefficient (measured as an elasticity) is comparable to other countries (see for instance Teulings and Hartog 1997).

In a different approach I could have discussed insider-outsider effects on the Dutch labour market and have stressed that generous welfare policies kept large parts of the potential labour force hidden away in long term unemployment and disability, isolated from the labour market and without any influence on necessary wage changes (Graafland 1990). I could have stressed the negative effects on supply and demand of labour of the sizeable wedge driven between labour costs and disposal earnings by taxes and social insurance premiums (Gelauff and Graafland 1994).

A web of restrictions?

Teulings and Hartog (1997) make the argument that the very corporatist labour market institutions lead to results in terms of productivity, wage growth and employment that would be the preferred outcome of neo-classical labour markets. A similar argument about the blessings of the welfare state for Dutch labour market performance can be found in a recent publication of the Ministry of Social Affairs (1996).

I could have contrasted the blessing of the corporatist setting with the arguments made by numerous Dutch economists complaining about the loss of labour productivity growth and welfare growth in recent decades (Nyfer 1996).

I learned from writing this article that it is quite possible and rather easy to make a case for the Dutch labour market being flexible - in spite of the fact that it is often believed to be sclerotic.

A case can always be made for both sides of the argument. It is rather easy to be a two armed economist. And it happens very often. There are many economic discussions that have at least two sides to it. Look at the (in)famous capital controversy between Cambridge UK and Cambridge USA, at the fierce discussions between Keynesians and Monetarists in earlier days or - to remain within Dutch boundaries - at the discussion about wage moderation whereby the Central Planning Bureau stresses the beneficial effects on employment of wage moderation while other economists stress the negative results in terms of welfare loss and lack of productivity growth.

Given that good argumentation rather than truth with a capital T is the mode of communication among economists and between economists and the world it is quite acceptable that many different views co-existed at the same time. There is a corollary to all this. It is about:

The art of being a forensic economist

Because at any time and at any moment many of the societal issues are not settled within economics but at least two sides can be taken on it, it is quite possible that different economists play different roles as expert witness in a social 'legal case'. I can very well imagine an economist defending the case *pro* minimum wages if hired as an expert witness by one party and defending the case *contra* minimum wages if called in by the other party.

Economists can be hired as a specialist in the arguments of each case, just as a lawyer can be hired by the defendant or his opponent. Economists are specialists in the art of economic rhetoric like lawyers are specialists in the art of legal rhetoric. Who is to judge? Society is to judge by weighting the force of the arguments which are given by each of the expert witnesses. In this 'law court of society', the policy makers could be the judges. But it should be clear that economists are playing a role as providers of arguments and not as providers of truth. But before it all goes too far I would like to stress:

5.3 The Art of Being Honest

Not all is rotten in the State of Economics. Rhetoric in economics does not lead to chaos and eternal loss if we allow for enough competition and openness in the scientific and societal discussions. With enough public discussion consensus can be built. With the increased possibilities of world-wide communication, difference of opinion between economists can be settled in the briefest of times.

Card and Krueger vs. the orthodox view on minimum wages
The Card and Krueger (1994 and 1995) attack on orthodoxy in the predicted effects of minimum wages is an illustration of this. In 1994 Card and Krueger published an article on the change of youth employment in fast food chains in New Jersey and Pennsylvania, after New Jersey had experienced an increase in the minimum wage and Connecticut not. They found not only that an increase in the minimum wage did *not* cause a decrease in employment but also that there was a case to be made for an increase in employment. Before Card and Krueger came onto the scene the consensus of mainstream economists was that minimum wages had a small but significant negative effect on youth employment. This consensus case was much influenced by the seminal Brown et al. (1982) review article in the *Journal of Economic Literature*. An enormous discussion followed and within months the orthodox view was re-instated. Card and Krueger by now have very much a lonely position in the area of minimum wages.[3]

Why was this discussion settled so fast? For various reasons. First of all there was a well-established consensus, based on many aspects of rhetoric. Second, the discussion was about a relatively simple issue, the size and significance of one single coefficient. This is very much different from more general policy discussions on the balance between the costs and benefits of the welfare state or on whether a more market driven health sector would create an increase in social welfare. Not all economic discussions can be settled in this way but quite a number of them can be pushed in the right direction by getting economists to agree on a narrow ballpark in which relevant economic coefficients and elasticities (demand and supply elasticities, substitution elasticities, reaction coefficients, and so on) would fall. To enhance this I would plead for much more replication and re-analysis in economics.

The need for replication and re-analysis
Replication and re-analysis of the claims of previous published work is very important as part of the methodology of rhetoric in

economics. There are five sources of differences in the estimates of parameters of interest for economic discussions:

- computational errors or different computer programs;
- different measurement or definition of variables;
- variation in the specification of estimating equations;
- variation in the specification of the econometric model and its stochastic properties; and
- different samples or sample selection of periods/observations.

One could say that there are two types of replication. One which I would call 'direct replication' in which a researcher using the same data set as the original researcher checks for the differences which occur because of the first four causes over the same sample. The second type, defined as 're-analysis' would use different data and throw light on the fifth issue. What is essential in the art of replication is that one explains the differences in the estimates of the same parameter of interest and attributes it to each possible source of difference.

The publish-or-perish system of rewards among economists is biased against replication. It is hard to get a replication of an existing article published. New ideas are easier to get published. This could change and can change if journals introduce a special section for replication and re-analysis of major empirical articles encouraging this line of research by guaranteeing publication under sensible conditions of submitted replication articles.[4]

5.4 Conclusion

If economists become masters in the arts of choosing the right model and of making a case, and develop enough competition and replication in their rhetorical search for the truth with a small t, we will be an asset to society and policy makers. All that remains for the policy makers is the art of picking the right economist or the economist who is right, whoever comes first.

Notes

1. For instance, utility maximizing consumer theory also leads to the testable hypothesis   that Slutsky matrices are negative semidefinite. This hypothesis is frequently falsified, yet this does not lead to dismissing utility maximizing utility theory.
2. Taken from: Snowdon, B., H. Vane, and P. Wynarczyk, *A Modern Guide to Macroeconomics: An Introduction to Competing Schools of Thought*, Aldershot, UK: Edward Elgar, 1994.
3. See the Review Symposium on the Card and Krueger book (1995) in the *Industrial and Labor Relations Review*, July 1995, 827-849, with contributions by Charles Brown, Richard Freeman, Dan Hamermesh, Paul Osterman and Finis Welch.
4. For example, *Labour Economics: An International Journal* published by North Holland will introduce such a replication and re-analysis section in its present volume.

PART II
CASE STUDIES IN POLICY ANALYSIS

6. Industrial Organization and Competition Policy: What Are the Links?

Alexis Jacquemin

At its most basic level, the aim of scientific activity is the comprehension of our world. Theories should be judged by how well they enable us to organize and understand our observations. This is especially true in the domain of industrial organization, where theory should provide a framework within which empirical research can be carried out.

The first part of this chapter presents the evolution of the analyses developed in the field of 'industrial organization' which has influenced criteria used in competition policy. As we shall see, the shift from the linear 'structure-conduct-performance' paradigm, primarily empirically based, to the 'new industrial organization' enshrined in game theory, has improved the quality of analyses in antitrust, but at a price. However, a reconciliation of the two approaches is currently both possible and desirable.

The second part of the chapter examines several market conducts that affect competition and for which European antitrust policy is expected to use criteria developed by old and new analyses in industrial organization. Three illustrations will be considered: concerted practices and parallelism of actions, co-operative R&D and cartel, mergers and efficiency defence. The first of these demonstrates the emerging influence of contemporary developments in economics; the co-operative R&D illustration provides an example of lax use of the efficiency defence; conversely, the merger regulation illustrates a strict approach, along with its dangers.

6.1   Industrial Organization and the Characterization of a Market

Market analysis, either from the point of view of the firm that operates or desires to operate in it, or from the viewpoint of the public authorities, requires proper characterization.

The principal objective of industrial organization has been precisely to provide this characterization, resorting to a scheme that relates the market structure with the behaviour of the economic agents who operate in it and with the performances that such a relation generates. Whether we refer to a manager of a firm or to a public authority responsible for antitrust policy, the fundamental problems are analogous.

At the level of market structure, industrial organization examines the number of competitors who operate in the relevant market and the distribution of market shares, the conditions of entry and exit, product standardization and its proximity to substitutable goods, the interdependence between upstream and downstream activities, the quality of information controlled by partners and the degree of risk involved.

As far as conducts are concerned, it should determine the respective role of price and non-price strategies, the level of co-operation which has been established over time among the various agents and the use of strategies of differentiation and diversification.

Finally, through the examination of performances - which deals with the allocation of resources or with actual profitability - the results obtained are evaluated.

A study so conceived that deals with structure, conduct and performances should, then, be able to provide an answer to a fundamental question: Which type of competition exists in this market?

The sense of the question varies according to who asks it. In the view of public authorities, the intention is to determine if the spontaneous forces of competition which characterize the market in question can or cannot lead to an efficient allocation of resources and a socially acceptable distribution of income.

However, from the firm's point of view, what counts is knowing if its own actual or potential relative position benefits sufficiently from market imperfections, in order to yield substantial and sustainable profits.

The many studies of industrial organization have applied a useful filter to this matter, permitting the identification and classification of some complex competitive phenomena of our industrial society. They have conferred substance to the famous 'empty box' of traditional microeconomic analysis.

The 'old' industrial economics

Nevertheless, until the 1960s for the most part, a dangerously reductive approach was adopted. It is worthwhile underlining at least two limits of the traditional industrial organization economics, one of a theoretical nature and the other of an empirical nature. On the theoretical ground, the analysis was seldom made in the context of a precise microeconomic model and rarely has the type of oligopolistic interdependence been made explicit. On the contrary, the accent has been placed on the description of the market structure and its direct links with the performances achieved.

From this viewpoint, industrial organization is a model in which change is treated as exogenous and where behaviour and performance are structurally determined. It is also a static system (or rather a comparative static one) that does not take into account that competition is an evolving and historic process with possibilities of retroactions, going, for instance, from performance to behaviour and from behaviour to certain structures that thus become endogenous.

On the empirical level, two types of study characterize the traditional outlook: case studies and econometric studies. Case studies, which were particularly prolific in the 1960s, have provided a better understanding of some industries and of some markets. The consideration of qualitative aspects has clarified the complexity of industrial reality, whereas quantitative measures, such as the degree of concentration or the profit rate, have provided simple summary indicators of the observed situation. These case studies, however, have not given rise to much hope that a general outline can be made and further developed.

After the 1960s econometric studies increased and set themselves the task of going beyond the limit of case studies by finding statistically significant links between some indicators of performance, such as the profit rate, and a whole set of indicators of market structure, in particular, the degree of concentration. These regressions have been based on cross sections of industries. Their objective is essentially to test simple hypotheses, possibly applicable to all markets, such as the existence of a linear relationship between the degree of concentration and the rate of profit in the industry. The theoretical arguments that are used to include or exclude a particular structural aspect from a list of explanatory variables are often *ad hoc*, made without clear reference to an underlying general model of which the tested equation is the reduced form. Moreover, the interpretation is a causal one - *ceteris paribus*, a high degree of concentration should result in a higher rate of profit - rather than an equilibrium relationship. The corresponding usual interpretation is the presence of market power in concentrated markets.

New industrial organization

What has come to be known as the 'new industrial organization' presents innovative methodological aspects. Moreover, on the basis of a more technical analysis, it has relaunched the eternal debate between those who see in our industrial economies an efficient adaptation to external conditions and those who see a search for market power (see Jacquemin, 1987).

Compared with earlier studies, recent research is increasingly using tools of microeconomic theory, models of imperfect competition, and game theory. Going beyond the extreme cases of perfect competition and monopoly, solution concepts grow in number. Oligopolistic interdependence has been explored by co-operative games as well as by models of noncooperative behaviour. Furthermore, dynamics in industrial structure have come to replace static approaches. Schumpeter (1950) has already stressed the intertemporal framework within which the competitive process should be placed.

We must assume that economic agents are making sequential decisions and taking into account the consequences of their actions on the subsequent evolution of industrial activity. Firms do not merely react to given external conditions, but try to strategically shape their economic environment by modifying, in a credible manner, market structure and market conducts of competitors. Then, the unidirectional causality, from structure through conduct to performance, breaks. For example, we have seen that, in the 'old industrial organization', super-normal profits in an industry would be associated with collusive behaviour brought about by high concentration possibly due to exogenous barriers to entry. In the new approach, the number of firms is determined endogenously and depends on the type of game being played by firms, defined in terms of choice variables (price, quantity and so on), timing of decision, and the number of replications of the game (Norman and La Manna, 1992). This approach also allows for the fact that buyers and sellers do not have a perfect knowledge of their partners or adversaries, their preferences, and their means. Situations of incomplete and asymmetric information are treated differently, and new concepts of equilibrium are again developed.

The role of modelling
A result of the new approach has been a proliferation of models, according to the choice of the strategy space, the firms' beliefs, the possibility of commitments, the temporal horizon, the attitude toward risk and asymmetries arising at each stage of the decision process. Several implications derive from these theoretical enrichments:

- The first is that the corresponding behaviours derived as optimal strategies at equilibrium demand high and growing levels of rationality.
- Furthermore, the number of possible equilibria for a given structure is generally large.
- A third aspect is that the solutions are not robust, for they are very sensitive to slight modifications in assumed initial conditions. At the very limit, any possible outcome can be rationalized, in particular by playing with information conditions.

In such a situation, economic experts involved in antitrust actions have a wide open field to attack or justify a given practice. 'Give me a result, I shall give you a theorem!' This explains recent criticisms made against the (ab)use of game theory. According to Milgrom and Roberts (1988, p. 450),

> in the economics of organization ... the vast bulk of the research has been primarily deductive theorizing ... too often the questions that the latest paper seeks to answer arise not from consideration of puzzling aspects of observed practices ... but from the desire to extend the analysis in an earlier paper that, in turn, may have been only tenuously connected to observation.

These criticisms are important but must not imply throwing out the baby with the bath water. What the rich panoply of possible models requires is a new combination of theoretical and empirical analyses. Rather than looking for *the* model which permits simple generalizations that can be applied to most industries, as previous authors would have liked, we must develop a menu of theoretical models from which the best adapted model to the market under study can be selected. On this basis, different views have been expressed. According to Fisher (1989, p. 119),

> the role of a generalizing theory is to tell us ... how conduct and performance depend upon structure. It may very well be the case that one cannot understand the history of the American rubber tire industry without knowing that Harvey Firestone was an aggressive guy who believed in cutting prices. The job of theory is to discover what characteristics of the rubber tire industry made such aggressive behavior a likely successful strategy.

However, Fisher adds: 'That question would be answered if we had a generalizing theory of oligopoly'. The following comment of Martin (1993, p. 564) is pertinent: 'A theoretical model tailored to the specific characteristics of the American rubber tire industry would answer the same question. Quite likely, it would supply the answer with greater clarity'. Contrary to monism, eclecticism is paradoxically close to the concern of losing, as a result of modelling, the qualitative richness of the information supplied by specific case studies of industry and markets.

Monism and eclecticism may in fact be complementary, in the sense that the model can be adapted to the major observed features of the industry. Beyond this, a richer typology of behaviour can be made to correspond to appropriate models. Indeed an important function of game theory is the classification of the multiple interactive decision situations. Just making the classification is already a form of science. 'The right classification is often the key to a successful theory. Modern biology was made possible by Linnaeus's classification of all living things into species and genera' (Aumann, 1985, p. 39).[1] By the same token, econometric studies based on inter-industry cross sections which are plagued by many problems of interpretation have been complemented by time series analyses of industry on the one hand and by intra-industrial comparisons on the other. Heterogeneity of economic agents, of their performance, and their strategies within the same industry can then be tested. More generally, game theory must be completed by a description of decision behaviour and empirical support. According to Aumann (1985, p. 65) 'Game-theoretic solution-concepts should be judged and understood in terms of the quality and quantity of their applications'. Indeed, neither theory nor empirics can stand alone, at least as regards the analysis of real-world industries.

From that point of view, the field of competition policy is a particularly important laboratory. It shows that competition policy must rely on sounder theoretical characterization than in the past but, simultaneously, that the diversity of models and results requires a case-by-case approach where insights into the ways firms acquire and maintain positions of market power become essential.

6.2   The Use of Industrial Organization in European Competition Policy: Some Illustrations

Differences in attitude and legislation about cartels and monopolies are evident from country to country. Several factors play a role. For example, contrary to large economies, small developed open economies having weak effects on the prices of traded goods maximize their real income level by a policy of free trade; and in this situation antitrust policy is not usually important given that international trade provides an effective source of discipline on market performance. In developing countries, on the other hand, the infant industry argument is often used for justifying protection against imports as well as the adoption of various forms of regulation restricting competition at home.

More profoundly, there are differences in attitudes toward economic power (private or public), freedom of contract and trade, efficiency and equity, that are grounded in dissimilarities in political, cultural and moral history, what Edwards (1967) calls the 'cultural inheritance'. For a long time in Europe, though competition has been considered desirable, it has not been accepted as an automatic selective device by which the fittest survive. Instead emphasis was put on the moral obligation in economic affairs: competition has to be fair. The predominant American view on the contrary has relied upon the interplay of selfish motives in competitive markets that Adam Smith's invisible hand is able to convert into public virtues. It is therefore not surprising that competition policy varies from country to country and over time. It is also expected that competition policy will be the result of forces different from the simple objective of promoting efficiency. In this field, political economy explanations could be as important for understanding public policy debates as economic arguments.

It is in that relativistic context that I shall present some illustrations of the European policy towards cartels and mergers. Through them, we shall see to what extent old and new economic criteria derived from Industrial Organization are utilized. Before that, a brief presentation of various objectives of competition policy will highlight the fact that the search of allocative efficiency is not the only criterion.

Goals of competition policy

Three main goals can be distinguished. The first one is the diffusion of private economic power, the protection of individual freedom and individual rights. Monopolies and cartels can then be seen as a radical departure from such individualism. It is in the light of these 'non-economic values' that Mestmacker (1980) has characterized the attitude adopted by the German authorities with respect to cartels before the Second World War. 'The Nazis', Mestmacker wrote,

> had shown how to transform a highly concentrated and cartelized economy into a central planning system ... Boycotts and collective discrimination were applied against outsiders in order to discipline them in the public interest. If the more traditional measures of economic coercion proved insufficient for the

purpose, even the formal transformation of private cartels into compulsory cartels was provided for after 1933. (Mestmacker, 1980, p. 388)

Mestmacker adds that acceptance of cartels was not limited to conservatives who cherished them as safeguards against the anarchy of free competition. Marxists also looked upon cartels and concentration as forerunners of rational socialist planning. He quotes Hilferding, who interpreted this development as tending towards 'a universal cartel, that is a rationally regulated society'! Conversely, the criterion of a diffusion of private economic power was originally basic to antitrust legislation and still occupies an important place, although perhaps more at the level of public opinion than at the policy level.

A second goal of competition policy distinct from a search of efficiency may be to protect the economic freedom of market competitors. Here the protection of competitors takes precedence over the defence of the competitive process as such. Attention is directed towards abusive practices such as coercion, discrimination, refusal to sell, boycotts, and cartels through which powerful firms might endanger the existence of weaker competitors. This type of approach is particularly in evidence in the national laws regarding 'unfair competition'. According to the Paris Convention of 1883, unfair competition is 'any act of competition contrary to honest practices in industrial or commercial matters'. The corresponding laws are intended to ensure that the competitors compete in a fair way, and carry out their social functions according to an ethical code of conduct. The standard of business ethics plays an important role in developing such a code of honest trade practices, but it is ultimately determined by the common sense of the courts.

The third type of competition policy goal is dear to the hearts of economists. Competition policy is one of the main instruments to ensure consumer welfare through both allocative and productive efficiency. One of the neatest affirmations of a purely efficiency-directed competition policy has been made by Bork (1967). According to his view, antitrust law must challenge inefficient conduct. A necessary (but not sufficient) attribute of inefficiency is a restriction of output beyond levels which would prevail under competitive conditions. Conduct not so identified must be presumed to enhance efficiency, and should not be the subject of legal sanction.

However, new research in industrial organization has shown that simple formulas for efficiency defined as net aggregate economic welfare (consumer surplus + producer surplus), appear to be deceptive and misleading. According to Tirole the theoretical foundations provided by game theory

> led many economists to reject the simplistic *Chicago view* of the world (based on perfect information) that price cuts are always natural responses to cost and demand shocks or to increased competitive pressure. (Tirole, 1989, p. 380)

More generally, with the various types of non-price competition, consumer welfare becomes more multi-dimensional and includes aspects such as the quality of the product, the speed and security of the supply and so on. Most of these aspects are not measurable and value judgments are necessary. An example is whether allocating a greater amount of resources to activities which result in technological change or product variation than would be allocated under a more 'classical' form of competition contributes enough to consumer welfare to outweigh the possible losses resulting from static inefficiencies. On the whole, a precise definition of the 'efficiency' criterion is more apparent than real and most of the time requires a delicate appreciation of complex trade-offs.

European principles

Three principles seem to have inspired the European authorities in this matter.

Although EC competition law encompasses many policy objectives and values, including distributive concerns, European authorities seem to have adopted the view that the rules of competition were not formulated to give protection to individual competitors but to uphold the competitive process. In its First Report on Competition Policy (1972, p. 17), the Commission wrote:

> Competition is the best stimulant of economic activity since it guarantees the widest possible freedom of action to all. An active competition policy makes it easier for the supply and demand structures continually to adjust to technological development. Through the interplay of decentralized decision-making machinery, competition enables enterprises continuously to improve their efficiency which is the *sine qua non* for a steady improvement in living standards. Such a policy encourages the best possible use of productive

resources for the greatest possible benefit of the economy as a whole and for the benefit, in particular, of the consumer.

Secondly, the idea is not to strive for the realization of perfect competition but to promote a 'workable competition', that is a process of rivalry under conditions of uncertainty that achieves a more efficient allocation of resources. This would ensure mobility of resources, the provision of alternative choices for producers and consumers and the use of the best economic practices in production and distribution. 'Workable competition' does not have the same solid theoretical foundations as perfect-competition theory and implies a value judgement from the political authorities; it simply describes market structures in which new technologies, organizational forms, preferences or products can arise and be developed without public or private restrictions.

A third principle is that competition is not the exclusive means of achieving the Community's goals. Other instruments may have to be used in situations 'when competition in itself is not enough to obtain the required results without too much delay and intolerable social tension'.[2] The choice between the alternative policies available, including industrial policy, must be based on their relative efficiency.

Finally, competition policy is viewed as the key instrument to achieve a genuine European market without internal frontiers.

Concerted practices and parallelism of actions
Article 85 of the Treaty of Rome states that:

> agreements between undertakings, decisions by associations of undertakings and concerted practices which may affect trade between Member States and which have as their object the prevention, restriction or distortion of competition within the Common Market shall be prohibited as incompatible with the Common Market.

Hence article 85 covers much more than formal cartel arrangements. It also embraces concerted practices, 'open-price' or information agreements. Such types of collusion without formal agreement may be expected to increase when cartel agreements are forbidden. The concept of concerted practices emerges most clearly in the celebrated

Dyestuffs case where manufacturers were accused of price collusion in the years 1964-1967.

In 1964, some ten producers sent telexes to their subsidiaries at almost exactly the same time, telling them to raise the prices of particular dyestuffs by a uniform rate of 14 per cent in Italy and in the Benelux. In January 1965, the increase was applied to West Germany.

In August 1967, a meeting of dyestuffs' manufacturers was held in Basel, Switzerland. One of them announced his intention of raising prices by 8 per cent in October. The other firms reacted by stating that the proposal would be considered. At the end of August, Geigy informed its agents and customers in several countries that prices would be raised. Other companies followed in September.

The accused companies defended themselves by stating that the *parallel action* was not concerted, but was based on the compelling force of the prevailing oligopolistic situation. In other words, the argument was that the companies could not have behaved otherwise because of the structure of the market. The defence also claimed that a firm which abstained from raising its prices could not have improved its market position because its competitors would have withdrawn their announced increases, and the profitability of all would have been impaired.

However, both the Commission and the Court pointed out that concertation of action had been in evidence: in 1964, telex messages in similar terms had stipulated equal price increases at exactly the same time. In 1965, and again in 1967, the facts belied the manufacturers' contention, and indicated gradual progressive co-operation between the firms concerned. With regard to the contention that an oligopolistic market structure compels firms to behave similarly, the response was that in the dynamic and uncertain conditions of real markets, this is not at all obviously true. In the Dyestuffs case there were several factors promoting intermittently competitive behaviour, such as the interchangeability of the standard colours, the different cost structure of manufacturers and the growing over-all demand for dyestuffs.

Since that first case, there has been a proliferation of similar situations where the Commission and the Court have had to distinguish between conscious parallelism of actions and concerted practices.

Simultaneously, game-theoretic contributions have made clear that collusive equilibria can be obtained without co-operation and direct communication: firms may only intelligently react to the actions of their competitors. The central concept is the 'Nash equilibrium' from which nobody has an interest to deviate because all players have adopted their best replies. In the context of non-cooperative repeated games, where firms never meet to communicate their strategies or to correlate their moves, it appears that a 'pacifist' attitude could lead everybody to more profitable equilibria than a aggressive one. This was already the intuition of Chamberlin (1933, p. 48) when he wrote:

> since the result of a cut by any one is inevitably to decrease his own profits, no one will cut and, although the sellers are entirely independent, the equilibrium result is the same as though there were a monopolistic agreement between them.

In recent years, the literature on the subject has been immense.[3] It has improved the identification of the structural factors that could hinder a collusive outcome that does not result from anticompetitive behaviour, such as a lack of market transparency, asymmetries among firms, dispersion of demand.

Simultaneously, many economists have attempted to measure equilibrium outcomes in markets that might be susceptible to tacit collusion. In these econometric studies, firm and industry conduct are viewed as unknown parameters to be estimated. For example, Slade (1987) has used daily time-series data on retail gasoline prices, sales, and unit costs, in a context of a price war. Demand, reaction function, and cost functions have been estimated. She was then able to test for tacit collusion and found support for profits higher than those implied by Nash behaviour in the one-shot game. More generally, the recent econometric studies of market power in single markets suggest that there is a great deal of market power in the sense of price-cost margins in concentrated industries (see Bresnahan, 1989).

As mentioned in the first part of this chapter, game literature on the theory of collusion has an embarrassment of richness, given the large range of possible collusive outcomes.[4] Consequently, it is difficult to select from such a vast multiplicity of equilibria. Furthermore, the results are sensitive to the conditions of information. For example, the distinction between collusion in homogeneous goods markets and heterogeneous goods markets is not confirmed by the theory: even large diversity between firms in some dimension may not be an impediment to achieving collusion. Heterogeneity among firms may, however, become an impediment to collusion when there is asymmetric information among firms about this heterogeneity.[5] For example, firms may have private information about their own costs, which is unobservable for competitors. In this case, it becomes a problem for firms to efficiently design cartel quotas.

At the empirical level, similar questions emerge. As an example, Porter (1983), in his study of the US railroad cartel in the 1880s, concluded that collusion had led to mark-ups consistent with static Cournot competition. However, Ellison (1994), working on the same data set and using a more careful model of the stochastic process driving demand, obtains the conclusion that prices were close to perfect collusion (quoted by Kühn and Vives, 1994).

In spite of these uncertainties about the robustness of the theoretical models and the enormous difficulties of obtaining the relevant statistical evidences, the European Court and the Commission are increasingly open to new economic analyses.

The Wood Pulp case illustrates such a move. According to the Judgment of the European Court (31 March 1993),

> since the Commission has no documents which directly establish the existence of concertation between the producers concerned, it is necessary to ascertain whether the system of quarterly price announcements, the simultaneity or near-simultaneity of the price announcements and the parallelism of price announcements as found during the period from 1975 to 1981 constitute a firm, precise and consistent body of evidence of prior concertation ... It is necessary to bear in mind that, although Article 85 of the Treaty prohibits any form of collusion which distorts competition, it does not deprive economic operators of the right to adapt themselves intelligently to the existing and anticipated conduct of their competitors.

The conclusions of the Court are clear:

It must be stated that, in this case, concertation is not the only plausible explanation for the parallel conduct.[6] To begin with, the system of price announcements may be regarded as constituting a rational response to the fact that the pulp market constituted a long-term market and to the need felt by both buyers and sellers to limit commercial risks. Further, the similarity in the dates of price announcements may be regarded as a direct result of the high degree of market transparency, which does not have to be described as artificial. Finally, the parallelism of prices and the price trends may be satisfactorily explained by the oligopolistic tendencies of the market and by the specific circumstances prevailing in certain periods. Accordingly, the parallel conduct established by the Commission does not constitute evidence of concertation. In the absence of a firm, precise and consistent body of evidence, it must be held that concertation regarding announced prices has not been established by the Commission.

Without referring specifically to the concept of Nash equilibrium, which was invoked by the defence and by the Advocate-General, the European Court, for the first time, has in fact utilized it.

In a very interesting comment, Kühn and Vives (1994), agree with the fact that, if information exchange would not raise the possibility of price fixing, it is hard to make a good economic case against it. But they argue that information exchange can be an independent infringement of Article 85(1). Their argument is based on the fact that the knowledge of industry characteristics required by the models to prove the existence of a tacit collusion is usually not available. For example, it is almost impossible to verify the type of demand and cost uncertainty that firms face in a particular industry.

In order to overcome these difficulties, the authors suggest forbidding as such some forms of information sharing, such as direct private information sharing on prices among producing firms, that facilitate the establishment of tacit collusion. This is in line with the new approach in industrial organization, according to which market conduct can transform market structure in order to reduce competition and make easier collusion. It also reflects the fact that given the complexities of the recent economic research in the field of tacit collusion, a pragmatic approach based on typologies can be useful.

Co-operative R&D and cartels

According to Article 85 para. 3 of the Rome Treaty, some collusive behaviour restricting competition in a non-minor way may be exempted because of sufficient beneficial effects. Four conditions are required :

- the agreement must contribute to the improvement of the production or distribution of goods or promote technical or economic progress;
- it must allow ultimate buyers a fair share of the resulting benefits;
- the restriction must be necessary for the attainment of the objective;
- the firms concerned must be unable to eliminate competition with respect to a substantial part of the product in question.

What Williamson (1977) calls a 'naive trade-off model' is a good way of illustrating these conditions. This model indicates that, in order to appreciate whether the cartel can benefit from the 'efficiency defence', it is sufficient to compare the surface corresponding to the 'deadweight loss', that is, the loss of consumer welfare created by the cartel, and the surface corresponding to its savings in resources which become available for alternative use.

This 'naive' static partial equilibrium model, with its cost-benefit analysis limited to two-dimensional terms requires a number of qualifications which strongly reduce its operationality. These qualifications include matters of timing, non-price competition, X-inefficiency, response of firms non-participating to the cartel and income distribution effects. What is in fact suggested by such a model is the difficulty of identifying precisely the efficiency consequences of business conduct and of advocating fine-tuned optimal antitrust roles. The conditions of article 85 para. 3 cannot rely on a strict welfare analysis and will often require compromise between conflicting and incommensurable values.

One way which has been used to reduce the burden of the trade-off is to implement Article 85 para.3, not so much on a case by case basis, but by granting group (or block) exemptions dealing with important types of agreements for which there exists a presumption that a situation of *market failure* can occur.

This system of exempting certain classes of agreements from the notification requirement avoids the necessity of a detailed analysis of each conduct. It creates codes of conduct that can increase the credibility of the policy and limit the discretionary power involved in the Article. At the same time, it preserves the Article's valuable message that antitrust policy must be sensitive to economies and that in some circumstances co-operative behaviour can restrict competition in a non-negligible way and still produce socially desirable results.

A clear illustration is the block exemption regulation of R&D agreements, which came into force in March 1985. To appreciate its content, it is necessary to examine in some depth the role of co-operative R&D.

The main arguments in favour of socially beneficial effects of co-operative research is based on a problem of market failure, bound to the appropriability of returns. The starting point is that the amount of research made by private firms and the diffusion of the knowledge generated by them may be socially inefficient over a broad range of market structure including competition. Two situations can be distinguished.

Assume first that there are no spillovers or externalities so that each firm's R&D influences only its own costs. Nevertheless, as long as firms in the pre-innovation market would not expect a perfect discriminating monopoly in the post-innovation market, appropriation of the entire social value from innovation will not be expected. Even the pre-innovation monopolist would not generally invest the socially optimal amount in R&D.

Now suppose that there are substantial R&D externalities or *spillovers*: the benefits of each firm's R&D flow without payment to other firms. This leads to underinvestment in R&D relative to the social optimum and to a structure of knowledge supply which is determined by the different degrees of appropriability of the various types. Incentives to innovate will also be reduced as the potential innovator knows that competitors will be freely strengthened by its own R&D investments. Some estimates of these positive externalities on other firms and industries put the social return on R&D at 20 per cent to 25 per cent, whereas the internal return is no more than 10 per cent to 12 per cent (Torre, 1990). The externalities have a geographical dimension too. Coe and Helpman (1993) conclude from a wide-ranging econometric survey that about a quarter of the benefits of R&D investment in the seven largest economies (the G-7) is appropriated by their trading partners.

It can then be argued that co-operative R&D can alleviate the following trade off. The incentives of a firm to do R&D requires a sufficient degree of appropriability of the benefits, and thus a limited diffusion of knowledge; but on the other hand a near-perfect appropriability (whether created by circumstances or policy) impedes spillovers of the results of R&D to other firms, at no-cost, and hence does not allow a sufficient decrease in aggregate R&D costs.

Co-operative R&D can then be viewed as a means of simultaneously internalizing the externalities created by significant R&D spillovers - hence improving the incentive problem and providing a more efficient sharing of information among firms. D'Aspremont and Jacquemin (1988) have used a model to study the impact of R&D spillovers on a firm's optimal R&D investment. In comparing the symmetric co-operative and non-cooperative solutions, they find that large spillovers lead to higher R&D expenditures and production levels under the co-operative scenario: this behaviour is superior from a social welfare point of view.[7]

Contrasting with these potential advantages of co-operative R&D, effects leading to a harmful reduction of competition must also be considered.

First, let us assume that it is feasible to limit the extent of the agreement solely to aspects of R&D and to exclude coordination at the level of the final product (pre-competitive level). The dangers of anticompetitive consequences are then strongly reduced. Still, one danger is that co-operative R&D could be a way for a dominant firm to avoid competition through innovation, by co-opting potentially very innovative rivals and by controlling and slowing down the innovation race (Reinganum, 1983). Coordinating the R&D process so as to avoid duplication can reduce initiative and lead to inflexibility and to waste in dead-end research, when multiple, not perfectly correlated research strategies could have been feasible. At the other extreme, incumbent firms with market power can, through concerted pre-emptive operations, excessively accelerate their programmes of R&D and innovation in order to exercise a dissuasive impact of potential entrants (Gilbert and Newbery, 1982).

A second situation involves an extended collusion between partners, resulting from their action in R&D and creating common policies at the product stage (competitive level). Discussions about R&D can for example spill over into illegal discussions on pricing policy. Co-operative R&D can also provide a ready mechanism for side payments in the sense that it is useful for cartel members to redistribute the revenues earned by the firms as a result of product market division. What makes these dangers probable is again the difficulty of appropriating technological breakthroughs. Partners who have achieved inventions want to control the processes and products which embody the results of their collaboration, in order to recuperate jointly, and as quickly as possible, their R&D investments. If the firms are prevented from such a joint exploitation and if the benefits of co-operative R&D are expected to be very quickly dissipated through intense product market competition, firms will be tempted either to avoid R&D co-operation and to maintain wasteful competition in the pre-innovation market or to use their co-operation to limit unduly their R&D. If this is true, a regulation of R&D co-operation excluding any co-operation at the level of the final markets could discourage or destabilize many valuable agreements. However, allowing an extension of co-operation from R&D to manufacturing and distribution encourages collusive behaviour which impedes competition.

Again, we may conclude that the models produced by the new Industrial Organization in this domain have improved the quality and the relevance of our analysis. Nevertheless, simultaneously, they have made the dilemma faced by the Antitrust Authorities more complex.

The text of the European Regulation 418/85 expresses the compromise that has been adopted. It covers joint research and development of products or processes and *joint exploitation of the results of that R&D.*

Art. 1(2)(d) specifies that 'exploitation of the results' means the manufacture of the joint venture product or the licensing of intellectual property rights to third parties. However joint marketing is not covered. An exemption could still have been obtained on the basis of Article 85 para. 3, following a notification. In 1990, the Commission granted such an exemption to the co-operation agreement on the research, development, production and *marketing* of certain electronic components for satellites, concluded by Alcatel (France), the second largest world manufacturer of communication equipment and systems, and ANT, one of the leading companies in Germany in the field of telecommunications.[8]

One of the arguments was that, in the particular field of satellites, the nature of demand means that the benefits of joint R&D and manufacturing can be obtained only if they are combined with some joint marketing. Finally, in 1993 (Regulation n° 151/93, OJ n°L021, 29/01/93), the 1985 Regulation was amended so as to extend cover to joint distribution of specialized products or products resulting from joint research and development. However, various conditions limit the exemptions.

By imposing conditions concerning the duration of the venture and the importance of the market share, the regulation aims to prevent agreements that might result in the elimination of competition in the relevant market. If the joint venture is of the conglomeral or vertical type, that is if the participants do not compete on the relevant product market, the exemption applies for five years, regardless of market share. If the joint venture is of the horizontal type, the exemption also applies for five years, but only if the parties' combined share of the relevant product market does not exceed 20 per cent. A comprehensive list of permissible clauses (the so-called white list) and prohibited (the so-called black list) is also included.

The main aspect of the Regulation is that the European authorities, confronted with the above dilemma, take into account the factors identified by economic analysis but adopt a pragmatic approach. They consider that co-operation in R&D, in many cases, cannot be limited to the sole level of pure R&D, and that it will generally lead to joint exploitation of the results in order to stabilize the agreements and to solve the appropriability problem. A priori, this approach has not a strong economic foundation given that external effects are more likely in basic, upstream research. But this could be challenged if one implies that R&D is an endogenized process, responding to the pressures of end users. Today this 'non-linear' view of the innovation process exercises growing influence on the European R&D policy (European Commission 1996).

Mergers and efficiency defence

Many economists give weight to the arguments that mergers and acquisitions are able to enhance efficiency by exploiting economies of scale and scope, learning economies, and also by improving the efficiency of management through the market for corporate control. However, the empirical evidence for this view is not strong. Coley and Reiton (1988) looked at US and British companies in the *Fortune* 250 list and the *Financial Times* 500 which in the past had made acquisitions to enter new markets. They conclude that only 23 per cent of the 116 firms analysed were able to recover the cost of their capital or, better still, the funds invested in the acquisition programme. It also appears that the higher the degree of diversification, the smaller the likelihood of success. For horizontal mergers in which the acquired firm is not large, however, the success rate is around 45 per cent. The main reasons for failure appear to be: too high a price paid for the acquisition, over-estimation of the potential of the acquired business in terms of synergies and market position, and inadequate management of the process of integration after the acquisition.

More generally, there is a striking contrast between ex ante event studies of the corporate mergers' potential gains and the ex post evaluations of the effective results. In his introduction to a special issue of the *International Journal of Industrial Organization* on 'mergers', Mueller (1989) concludes that prior to the mergers the shares of acquiring firms tend to outperform the market. At the time of the announcement, there is little change in the acquiring firm's share price. The post-acquisition performance of acquiring company share prices is below their pre-merger performance, and in many studies below that of the market. This post-merger performance matches the constant or declining performance of the acquired units measured in profitability, market shares or productivity. 'This pattern appears to be characteristic of mergers in the United States over at least the last 60 years, and probably the last century. It also appears characteristic of mergers in Europe and Japan.'

This suggests that, in many cases, there is no real trade-off between efficiency gains from mergers, notably in the form of cost reductions and an increase in monopoly power, because in the first place efficiency gains are simply not there. Still there are situations where the trade-off can be relevant.

In that case, the antitrust authority has the task of deciding whether efficiencies outweigh the increased risk of collusion. Indeed a horizontal merger reducing the number of independent firms permits coordinated use of previously independent productive assets (capital, patents, trademarks and so on) and increases concentration in the relevant market. This can lead to higher prices.

At this stage, we again meet the situation created by the development of economic analysis. On one hand, industrial organization economics has improved the criteria and the tools that can be used for evaluating the effects of a merger. However, on the other hand, the new dimensions to be taken into account are very complex and sensitive, and the information that antitrust authorities possesses is generally inadequate to permit a full-blown cost-benefit analysis.

Examples

Two important examples, calling into question the 'naive' trade-off analysis mentioned in the previous section, support that view.

The first one concerns the static case. Farrel and Shapiro (1990) provide a model where they analyse the output and price effects of a merger among Cournot oligopolists, emphasizing the effects on nonparticipant firms. Their main contribution is an identification of the role of the response of these nonparticipant firms, to any output reduction by the merging parties. If nonparticipating firms reduce their output, the merger may well lower welfare even though it is profitable. On the contrary, if nonparticipant firms with large mark-ups expand their output noticeably in response to the merger, a significant welfare gain can be provided.[9] More generally, a merger's effect on total welfare is made of three components: the change in joint profits of the merging firms, the change in profits of the nonparticipant firms and the change in consumers' surplus.

Could this notable improvement in the identification of the effects of mergers lead automatically to a better merger policy? In their reply to a comment by Werden (1991), Farrell and Shapiro (1991) adopt a prudent attitude and underline three limitations of their analysis:

- 'whether or not the Cournot model is helpful for merger policy is very hard to know ex ante: clearly the assumptions are false, but it is much less clear whether they are false in such important ways that the conclusions are misleading';
- the analysis 'relies heavily on the assumption of homogeneous products' and
- 'the Cournot model ignores the possibility of explicit collusion'.[10]

And they conclude:

> it would shock us ... if the Department of Justice and the Federal Trade Commission were to decree that, henceforth, proposed mergers should be analyzed solely using the Farell-Shapiro model.

It remains that their analysis could contribute to a better antitrust policy toward mergers.

A second illustration of the limits of the traditional 'trade-off' concerns the dynamic effects of a merger. Ordover and Baumol (1988), in their analysis of mergers in high-technology industries, conclude that mergers in high-technology industries, in which technologies and products are short-lived, should raise fewer concerns than similar mergers in industries which have entered their stable phase. This suggestion holds as long as high-technology mergers do not combine firms with large shares of substitute R&D assets that also require large shares of market specific assets for their effective exploitation. On the whole the message here is that, when there is a trade-off between static and dynamic efficiency, it is wise to favour the long-run dynamic performance that is expected to ultimately overcome any static loss.

Still, the existence of such a trade-off can be questioned. Some evidence suggests that R&D is not characterized by substantial economies of scale and that monopoly power can be expected to inhibit R&D and technological advance in the long run. Furthermore, avoiding wasteful duplication, internalizing external effects and

ensuring a large dissemination of knowledge could be obtained
through less dangerous devices than full mergers, such as R&D co-
operation at the 'precompetitive stage'. What can be effectively
argued, in the application of merger policy, is that in industries
characterized by short-lived high-technology and rapidly expanding
demand, all other things being equal, the prospect of efficiency gains
is enhanced and the danger of monopoly power is limited.

It is in that context that we shall look at the European Regulation
of mergers. The absence of such a control provision was, for a long
period, a major gap in EC competition policy. The Commission
finally succeeded in getting the Council of Ministers to adopt a
Regulation in December 1989. It applies to mergers having a
Community dimension as defined by a combination of criteria relating
to total turnover and geographical distribution of turnover within the
Community - aggregate worldwide turnover must exceed Ecu
5,000 million, and aggregate EC turnover of each of at least two
firms has to exceed Ecu 250 million.

As we have seen, considerations of efficiency are expected to
enter into merger appraisal. For example, under the 1984 revision of
the US Guidelines, mergers likely to raise prices will be permitted if
the parties can demonstrate by 'clear and convincing evidence' that
the merger is 'reasonably necessary' to create significant cost savings
or other efficiency benefits.

In contrast, the European Regulation has adopted a strict
approach: the wording suggests that the regulation contains no
defence similar to the one stated in Article 85 para. 3 for cartels, and
that effective competition is the only reference. The wording also
implies that only the consumers' surplus, and not the producers'
surplus, is retained: apparently some sacrifice of consumer interest
for the sake of higher profits is not accepted.[11]

It is hard to believe that in practice such a strict policy will be
fully implemented and that the role of potential efficiency gains will
be ignored.

In fact, the danger is that instead of an explicit cost-benefit
analysis, surreptitious compromises would be sought within the
Commission. This already appears in the first negative decision taken
by the Commission. In that case, it prohibited the acquisition of
de Havilland, a Canadian subsidiary of Boeing, by Aérospatiale of

France and Alenia of Italy. The Commission argued mainly that the merger would have given de Havilland and ATR (the Franco-Italian joint venture) 50 per cent of the world market and 67 per cent of the EC market for commuter aircraft with 20 to 70 seats. This would have created a dominant position, affecting even the largest producers (such as British Aerospace and Fokker), with no competition from the United States or Japan. Whatever its specific merits and problems (especially the definition of the relevant market), it can be argued that this decision is important: even in a 'special' sector such as aerospace, the Commission seems to stick to the principle that mergers and takeovers should be judged purely on competitive grounds.

However, there are some ambiguities about the role of economies in the decision. Having established that the ATR/de Havilland merger would lead to a reduction in competition, the Commission states: 'without prejudice as to whether cost saving consideration are relevant for the assessments under article 2 of the Merger regulation, such cost savings would have a negligible impact on the overall operations of the ATR/de Havilland, amounting to around 0.5 per cent of the combined turnover'. According to Jenny (1992, p. 95),

> this decision offers some solace to the economists in that, although the Commission refuses to say explicitly whether productive efficiency gains are relevant for considering whether or not a merger is compatible with the common market, it nevertheless does discuss the importance of the manufacturing cost reductions alleged by the parties in a way that, at least implicitly, suggests that productive efficiency gains must be compared to the potential losses of consumer surplus due to the increase in concentration brought about by the merger.

In another decision on the acquisition of NCR (a computer manufacturer) by ATT (January 1991), the Commission seems to go further and argue that the merger could have been illegal because it would yield economies, and hence create or strengthen a dominant position. Its conclusion was that the potential advantages which ATT hopes to gain from this concentration are for the moment theoretical and have yet to be proved in a future market place. This suggests that had the Commission believed that the merger was likely to contribute to economic progress, it would have considered opposing it.

An implication of such a situation is that a strict and apparently rigorous approach emphasizing the preservation of effective competition could lead to perverse effects according to which subreptice compromises between competition policy and industrial policy are made (see Buigues, Jacquemin and Sapir, 1995).

6.3   Conclusion

The complexity of human behaviour is especially evident in the world of economics and corporate strategies. In this domain, simple mechanic laws and repetitive processes lose part of their relevance as a result of strategies that transform and manipulate the existing environment. Productive and organizational structures are not simply the outcome of some sort of natural necessity. They result largely from deliberate choices.

In this context, Industrial Organization economics has, over time, elaborated important concepts, models and typologies that reveal the richness of corporate conducts. Simultaneously, however, it is far from an exact science, and its results remain fragile.

Implications for the regulators, and more specifically the Antitrust Authorities, are ambiguous. On the one hand, they can rely on the new theoretical and empirical analyses, to the extent that they identify more and more effectively the diverse characteristics of our real industry economy. On the other hand, the very limited information at the disposal of these authorities and the difficulty in coping with complex tradeoffs, especially for the Court, constrain the effective use of the new knowledge.

Our illustrations of the European policy towards concerted practices, co-operative R&D and mergers have shown how the Commission and the Court are trying more and more to adopt a workable approach, combining 'science' and pragmatism, relying on presumptions and shortcuts that reflect current economic knowledge and beliefs.

An important implication of this approach is that the 'experts' involved in a case are expected to be modest. As Schmalensee (1987) wrote, 'economists cannot testify with the confidence of experts on ballistics and fingerprints', and, we may add, even if they are very well paid.

Notes

1. Aumann also writes that 'it is somewhat surprising that our disciplines have any relation at all to real behaviour'!
2. *First Report on Competition Policy*, 1972, p. 17.
3. For surveys, see Shapiro (1989), Jacquemin and Slade, (1989) and, more recently, Baker (1993).
4. According to a 'Folk theorem', under general conditions, repetition of any individually rationale outcome in the stage game can be supported as a supergame equilibrium with sufficiently little discounting.
5. Another important aspect is the asymmetric information between the antitrust authorities and the firms which have the relevant data on costs and consumer demand (principal-agent relationship). See Besanko and Spulber (1989), who consider the optimal design of antitrust policy when collusive behaviour is unobservable and production costs are private information. See also Smets and van Cayseele (1995) who explore the best division of competence between national and supranational antitrust authorities, when these authorities are affected by asymmetric information.
6. In fact, in competitive markets with homogeneous products, equilibrium prices must be uniform, in spite of different costs. Similarly, differences in price elasticities across regions lead to less price discrimination in case of competition than with collusion.
7. These results have been generalized. For references, see d'Aspremont and Jacquemin (1990).
8. EC Commission, *XXth Report on Competition Policy*, 1991.
9. Let us recall that, in a Cournot equilibrium, large mark-ups are associated with large market shares, and large firms have lower marginal costs.
10. Another limit has been identified by Barros and Cabral (1994). They analyse the case of an open economy where the regulator is only concerned with domestic welfare, that is, the impact on consumers and domestic firms. One of their conclusions is that the criterion proposed by Farrell and Shapiro should not be followed 'literally' in such a case.
11. Assuming that a merger must be profitable for the firms that are willing to be part of it, this implies that an increase of the sum of the consumers' surplus and profits by firms not participating is not a sufficient condition for allowing a merger

7. Why Does Economics Only Help with Easy Problems?

Thomas C. Schelling

My title is only partly facetious, and is not intended to denigrate the science - or art? - of economics itself, but rather to observe how little difference economic analysis appears to make in most important policies. My observations are all from the United States, and in a few instances I am sure are unique to the United States. And I shall use 'economic analysis' to imply policy analysis, including the decision sciences, systems analysis, operations research, statistics and econometrics, and 'implementation analysis'. I begin with a litany of issues to which policy analysis in the United States appears to have had little or no impact.

Abortion

Abortion was a quiescent issue politically until twenty five years ago. For reasons I do not think anyone has yet adequately explained, abortion suddenly leaped into public consciousness, a few states drastically changed their anti-abortion laws, and the courts quite suddenly reversed nearly a century of tradition. What would have happened had only the legal status of abortion been reversed, I find hard to predict retrospectively, but what did happen was that the issue of public financing of abortion arose in the context of publicly financed medical care; and on that issue the traditional opposition to abortion, which had been caught unorganized and surprised by the court decisions, rallied to counterattack. Where this will eventually all come out, it is still too early to tell. There are a few studies that empirically demonstrate what is already plausible to an economist, namely, that the public financing of abortion had comparatively little to do with the ease and frequency with which abortions would be obtained. The most recent study I have seen indicates that for the

United States neither the price of abortion nor Medicaid financing of abortion has a substantial impact on the number of abortions. Public funding, even funding in foreign-aid programs, is a favourite issue on both sides of the abortion debate, possibly for reasons independent of the economic analysis; but in any case nobody is listening to the analysis.

Race relations

At least since the election of John F. Kennedy, no policy issues in the United States have been more divisive, more loaded with hope and tragedy, than relations between the races, especially between 'whites' and 'blacks'. The defining moment was probably the Supreme Court decision in 1955 requiring the desegregation of public schools. Recently what some call 'affirmative action' and others call 'reverse discrimination', pervasive in Federal contracting, college education, and labour relations, is now under severe attack. Issues of race overlap the issues of poverty, crime, and fatherless households. There was one moment of triumph for policy analysis when a study group produced a report that was used successfully before the Supreme Court in arguing that segregation by race, independently of the correlation between the race of the students and the quality of the schools, could impair educational outcomes. Since that time it is hard to find policy choices at any level of government that were substantially driven by analysis of the alternative outcomes that could be expected from alternative policies. The recent furore over the book by Herrnstein and Murray (1994), *The Bell Curve*, casts doubt not only on whether their results can stand up to criticism, but whether certain policy issues can ever be treated analytically without generating as much hysteria as analytical interpretation.

Illegal drugs

Policy toward illegal drugs is another area apparently immune to analysis. On the issue of somewhat relaxing the penalties for possession of marijuana there is now the experience of a dozen states that drastically relaxed their laws on that subject a decade and a half ago. There have been some studies, somewhat equivocal in their results, on whether the relaxation spurred consumption. They are never cited in debate. There are studies of the effect of clean-needle programs on the spreading of AIDS, but clean needles a decade ago became a litmus test of whether one is serious about the drug problem. The issue of what is usually called drugs 'legalization', which is not literally what most of its proponents have in mind, cannot even be raised in public by a senior government official without a resulting clamour for resignation. This policy area is substantially impervious to analysis.

Crime and punishment

Crime and its punishment, of which drugs are a large part, are susceptible to analysis. A popular proposal has recently been the one referred to as 'three strikes and you're out'. Three felony convictions are to be followed by life imprisonment without benefit of parole. There have been studies of the cost, including medical care, of keeping a forty-five-year-old prisoner locked up for another thirty-five or forty years, compared with the likely committing of violent crimes by the middle aged and the elderly, but in the policy debate there is so little interest that even newspapers don't bother reporting the analytical results. Some ingenious polls have demonstrated that people who like capital punishment believe in its efficacy as a deterrent and people who dislike capital punishment dispute its value as a deterrent, and both sides formulate their positions with great attention to the deterrent effect or its absence, but neither side appears interested in the evidence. A related issue, gun control, appears unrelated to any analysis of what kind of gun control might lead to what kind of result. Interestingly, people who tend to believe in gun control are often against legal controls on marijuana, because the marijuana laws cannot possibly be enforced; people who favour heavy penalties on the use of marijuana usually object to gun control on grounds that laws against possession of guns could not be enforced.

Health care

Policy toward health care looks like a promising field for the application of economic analysis. It involves market incentives, demography, public support for medical schools, regulation of prescription drugs, income taxation of employer-provided health insurance, mandatory insurance in the workplace, *etcetera*. The

President of the American Economic Association, Professor Fuchs, said in his 1996 presidential address that there has been a thirteen-fold increase in the number of PhDs in health economics in the last thirty years; nevertheless, he concludes, the health care debate of 1993-94 in the United States, a debate that led nowhere, reflected little influence of the health economists. I will have more to say later about his explanation for why that was so.

Budgetary policy
Balancing the budget has consumed more time and energy on the part of presidents, senators, congressmen, high level budget officials, and presidential candidates than any other subject for the last several years. The subject might have led to the first constitutional amendment in decades; and no candidate for congressional office, let alone for the presidency, could dare to question the wisdom of balancing the federal budget. Why an exactly zero deficit should be so compellingly attractive surely has nothing to do with economic analysis. Probably, like clean needles in the war on drugs, a 'little deficit' in the war on the deficit is interpreted as a lack of seriousness, or as the equivalent of one little drink to a reformed alcoholic. Economists even outside the federal government have been remarkably silent on this during the past three years, I suppose because they perceive that a full page ad in the *New York Times* would not receive attention worth the cost of the ad. And lately in the 1996 presidential campaign the flat tax, the centrepiece of Mr. Forbes's platform, for a while won a popularity contest with neither help nor hindrance from most of the economics profession, largely, I suppose, because they were caught by surprise.

Finally, the 'new revolution' in American politics, reversal of the growth of federal responsibility and devolution of responsibility and authority to the states - 'back to the states' as it was erroneously referred to - appeared to be popular not only because the Federal Government has become a popular scapegoat but because of the 'self evident' principle that state governments, closer to the people, can do a better job, and do it with a less expensive superstructure than the Federal Government. The truth of this hypothesis, considering how much hinges on it, would have deserved careful historical, empirical, and theoretical study. But that would have taken time, and politics often can't wait. Furthermore, it isn't at all clear that anybody would care whether that particular argument for devolution to the states had any validity. An indication of the lack of depth in this reasoning is that the argument almost always ran in terms of what governors wanted and what governors could do, rather than state legislatures.

There is one area of policy in the United States that has been exceptionally responsive to analysis. That is defence policy, which I will come to shortly. First let me draw on Professor Fuchs's assessment of why economics has had so little impact on the health care debate, and generalize what he has to say to the numerous policy arenas that I have mentioned.

7.1   Health Policy

Fuchs administered a questionnaire to the health economists 'whom I considered to be the leading people in the field, plus some of the more promising recent PhDs. There were 46 respondents (response rate 88 percent)' (Fuchs, 1996, pp. 6-7). He asked twenty questions, and asked three experts from three different universities to identify which of the twenty questions were relatively 'value-free' ('positive' questions), and which had substantial value aspects ('policy-value' questions). Their independent replies, he reports, were almost unanimous in identifying seven as 'positive' and thirteen as 'policy-value'. Each question was in the form of a statement with which the respondent could agree or disagree.

Positive questions were such as, 'The primary reason for the increase in the health sectors share of GDP over the past 30 years is technological change in medicine', or 'third-party payment results in patients using services whose costs exceed their benefits, and this excess of costs over benefits amounts to at least 5 percent of total health care expenditures.' Policy-value statements were such as, 'The U.S. should seek universal coverage through a broad-based tax with implicit subsidies for the poor and the sick,' and 'Insurance companies should be required to cover all applicants regardless of health condition and not allowed to charge sicker individuals higher premiums.'

What Fuchs found, so plausible in retrospect but what I might not have guessed, is that leading health-care economists in the United States, though not quite unanimous, produced a strong consensus on the positive questions. The answers to the two that I mentioned were agreed to by 81 and 84 per cent, respectively. The policy-value questions found no such consensus. Only one of the thirteen questions had substantially more than two-thirds of the health-care economists agreed on the answer; on virtually all of the answers they divided close to 50-50 or within the range of two to one.

Fuchs's interpretation is that policy judgements are heavily dependent on values, and even people as similar in professional training and background as health-care economists, who can agree 80 or 90 per cent on the positive questions, are split on the policy (value) questions. The value questions were almost entirely normative in expression: of the thirteen policy-value questions, nine contained the word 'should' and the other four contained 'inequitable', 'is desirable', 'inefficient', or 'greater than is socially optimal'.

Values

There is a widespread judgement in the United States that economists, especially 'mainstream' economists, are remarkably alike in their values, in what they take for granted, in their attitude toward markets, efficiency, and the use of incentives. And I do not dissent from that judgement. Furthermore, the health-care economists that I know, and I know a great many, do not seem to me to be heterodox in their methodology or dissident from the mainstream. It is remarkable to me that they could show such a powerful consensus on the positive statements - statements on which the economic theorists, who were also offered the same questions, differed drastically in at least two cases, suggesting that the 'correct' responses were not self evident - yet differ so widely on the policy prescriptions.

Before I heard Professor Fuchs I was going to conclude that the reason why economic analysis appears so impotent on so many big issues was that on those big issues it is values that predominate, not analysis. But I was also going to say that even on policy issues in which values predominate, economic analysis should be of help. My undergraduate students often choose policies according to the values they attach to the *outcomes* they anticipate, and they often anticipate outcomes wrong. I try to persuade them that they should keep their values on hold while they work through the analysis; then, when they have thought their way through to a correct anticipation of outcomes, it is time to apply their values. Students initially have strong reactions to issues like rent control, gasoline rationing, cash versus in-kind assistance, minimum-wage laws, electric-utility regulation, farm price supports, and tariffs; they often - American students, at any rate - favour or oppose a policy because it helps or hurts 'the poor'. If I can get them to withhold judgement until we have worked out the theoretical ramifications, and discovered who gains, who loses, and maybe how much, they can then bring their values out of storage and use them more wisely.

But Professor Fuchs provides powerful evidence that the problem is not that economists cannot get heard on the policy issues on which they have expert judgement; it is that they differ among themselves on the value-laden policy judgements.

I have been asked to discuss the role of policy analysis in environmental policy. I shall in a moment, and I shall report that policy analysis has not only contributed little, but has often been overtly excluded. But first, a policy area where analysis has had an impact.

7.2   Defence Policy

I was recently asked to lecture on the influence of academia on US National Security Policy. In preparing the lecture I convinced myself that, in a manner probably unique to the United States, academic research had been not only more influential in defence policy than in any other policy area, but strikingly so. I shall describe that influence and make a few guesses about why that has been so.

Until the Second World War, military policy in my country, and especially the military services themselves, were virtually insulated from academia or anything intellectual. The subject of military strategy barely existed on any university campus before the Second World War. This situation changed immediately after the War. The Air Force established the forerunner of the RAND Corporation in 1946; it was incorporated as a not-for-profit research organization in California in 1948, had substantially independent command over a large research budget, and was deliberately kept out of the Washington area so that it could work on the long range issues of its own choice rather than be available for quick answers to immediate questions. When Sputnik flew, in 1957, the RAND Corporation was the only source of information about possible earth-satellite orbits.

By the late 1950s strategic studies, mainly concerned with nuclear weapons policy and European alliance policy, had bloomed at many universities and think tanks, and through the 1960s the ideas generated in academia became powerfully influential in US policy. I want briefly to survey the various channels and media through which ideas originating in academia found their way into policy. Mainly, but not entirely, the ideas penetrated the executive branch rather than the Congress, and in most policy areas it is not sufficient for ideas to be adopted in the executive branch. If the Department of Health and Human Services, or the Department of Housing and Urban Development, or the Department Transportation, succumbs to policy ideas that originate in academia, the Congress is demonstrably capable of ignoring those ideas. The Congress is always much less likely to ignore policy ideas put forward by the Department of Defense, especially when there is no split between the civilian leadership and the senior officers of the uniformed services.

People
Beginning with the Kennedy Administration in 1961 an obviously potent medium through which academic influence could penetrate into the American defence establishment was the appointment of academic people to senior positions. President Kennedy's national security advisor was MacGeorge Bundy, Dean of Arts and Sciences at Harvard, and Bundy's deputy was another Harvard professor. MacNamara, Kennedy's Secretary of Defense, had an M.B.A. from Harvard and appointed four academics as assistant secretaries. An MIT professor became Director of the State Department Policy Planning Staff; a Harvard Law School professor became General Counsel of the State Department.

These people brought not only the concrete ideas they had developed or learned in academia, but an academic bent for analysis, a culture they shared with other academics, and personal acquaintances back in academia. They all became channels for ideas from academia and they drew on former colleagues to serve on advisory boards and committees.

Eight years after Kennedy's election President Nixon introduced Dr. Kissinger to his television audience as his new National Security Advisor. Kissinger's entire career, except for a stint in the army, had been academic. Generally Republican administrations have not used academics on the scale of the Democrats, but Kissinger's deputy (later President Bush's national security adviser), Scowcroft, was a military officer with a PhD in international relations.

Carter's national security adviser was an academic, as was his Secretary of Defense. And in the Clinton Administration a congressman with a PhD became Secretary of Defense and immediately nominated at least five academics to the rank of assistant secretary or higher. One of them now directs the Central Intelligence Agency.

People - academic individuals - appointed to senior policy positions give the American defence-policy establishment a porosity, a permeability, a penetrability to academic ideas that is surely unique among the governments of the world.

Institutions
But that is not all. The military services themselves operate four major 'war colleges', nine-month academies for the advanced education of people on the verge of becoming admirals and generals. The senior one is the National War College in Washington DC. It takes each year roughly 50 from the Army, 50 from the Navy, 50 from the Air Force, and 50 from civilian agencies together with a few from Canada and other NATO countries. Most of the curriculum is government and politics, diplomacy, international economics, and military strategy. The faculty is half to two-thirds civilian, some permanent and some invited in for a year or two; the rest of the faculty is recruited from among the more outstanding students. Lectures are mainly by government officials and invited academics. Additionally the Army, Navy, and Air Force have their own war colleges of comparable size.

These war colleges have a serious academic atmosphere. My first experience was in 1959, when I lectured at the Air War College. At that time the colonels in the audience were people who had either gone into the Army Air Corps in World War II straight out of high school or had interrupted their college and never returned. Few in the class of 1959 had a bachelor's degree. The student body was not entirely receptive toward civilians from college campuses who wanted to talk to them about war, mobilization, military economics or alliance politics. A dozen years later demography had run its course, the entire student body had the equivalent of a bachelor's degree, at least a third had higher degrees in management, economics, international relations, or engineering, and some had PhDs.

There were two other academic programs for military officers. One was to send officers at the rank of colonel or navy captain to centres for advanced study like the International Institute for Strategic Studies in London, the Council on Foreign Relations in New York, the Harvard Center for International Affairs, or the MIT Center for International Studies. These people spent an academic year in an academic environment. The other was a vigorous PhD program, more active in the Army and the Air Force than in the Navy. In my thirty years at Harvard I had at least thirty young officers getting PhDs in political economy, government and politics, or economics.

One consequence of this development over the past 40 years or so is that the sharp distinction that once existed between the uniformed and non-uniformed policy people in the Pentagon has been substantially smoothed over. There was a time, early in the Kennedy Administration and continuing for a while into the Johnson Administration, when there were reported cultural incompatibilities between senior military officers and younger civilian 'whiz kids' in the Department of Defense. But, healthily, the main reaction of the military services was to see that their own people got the kind of training that would allow them to hold their own with their civilian counterparts.

The question arises, why should 'values' obstruct consensus on health economics but not on nuclear strategy. I can only conjecture. Perhaps it was the sheer novelty and unfamiliarity of the nuclear challenge. A little history may help. Three books appeared in 1961 that epitomized an emerging consensus on what arms control should be about. Each was a group effort, and each stimulated discussion while being written. During the summer of 1960 Bull's manuscript,

The Control of the Arms Race (Bull 1961), was circulated by the Institute for Strategic Studies in preparation for that institute's second annual conference. That same summer a study group met on the outskirts of Boston, and Halperin and I produced a little book (Schelling and Halperin 1961), discussed at numerous meetings of the Harvard-MIT Seminar on Arms Control during the fall of 1960, reflecting what we took to be an emerging consensus, one that was wholly consistent with the ideas that developed around Hedley Bull's manuscript at the ISS. And that same year Brennan organized a conference that generated *Arms Control, Disarmament, and National Security* (Brennan 1961). Participants in this activity were the White House national security adviser of the new Kennedy Administration, the White House science adviser, the assistance secretary of defense for international security affairs, the assistant secretary for policy planning in the State Department, and many others. Unquestionably the ABM Treaty, that was ratified in 1972, was a direct outgrowth of those studies.

If military policy is the area that has been most receptive to policy analysis in general, and economic analysis in particular, my assigned topic - environmental policy - may be at the opposite extreme.

7.3   Environmental Policy

In environmental regulation, the need for economizing ought to be beyond dispute. Together the costs incurred in the Federal Government's budget and the costs imposed by regulation on farm, industry, and local government are estimated in the neighbourhood of a quarter of a trillion dollars annually, without counting prospective huge costs of cleaning up after 50 years of nuclear materials production. Just getting the priorities straightened out could be enormously valuable, yet for cleaning up toxic waste the Department of Defense, the Department of Energy, and the Environmental Protection Agency recently had, and probably still have, altogether different philosophies of priority.

The two main contributions of economic analysis should be, I expect, the design of procedures for comparing benefits with costs, especially at the margin, and the design of incentives to substitute for direct regulation of technology. Why have economists been so unsuccessful for a quarter century in getting acceptance of these ideas at least in principle? I can see at least two reasons.

One is that much environmental regulation, as well as regulation of safety in the workplace, is, or is perceived to be, about saving lives, that is, about preventing deaths. Life and death are a subject that many people, including legislators and administrators, believe should not be contaminated by cost considerations.

The second reason is that, at least until recently, most environmentalists in the United States, including those on the staffs of congressmen, chose to treat pollution as a criminal activity, not an activity to be governed through the marketplace. Effluent charges were despised as 'licenses to pollute'.

The American Congress has passed a number of laws that overtly prohibit regulators from achieving a reasonable relationship between the costs of their actions and the benefits. The most publicized example is something called the Delaney Amendment, enacted under the Federal Food, Drug and Cosmetic Act, which bans any substance (except tobacco) that has been proven carcinogenic at any dosage in any animal test. This provision has survived even the great hullabaloo that occurred when the Food and Drug Administration declared that Diet Coke could not contain saccharine. In many cases brought by environmentalist organizations the Courts have ruled that regulatory decisions had wrongly allowed costs to be taken into account.

In cleaning toxic waste sites any explicit criteria relating to risk tend to be extremely conservative. A commonly proposed standard is that the 'most exposed person' should incur no more than one-in-a-million lifetime risk of death. And this without regard to cost.

On the matter of incentives, I received an inquiry from a former student who was in the Environmental Protection Agency's Office of External Research, in the late 1970s. He wanted to know why it was that nearly all economists believed that environmental regulation could be most efficiently handled through market incentives, and hardly anybody but professional economists did - not legislators, not administrators, not environmental lobbyists. I took his money and financed four studies of which one was an opinion survey. The researcher interviewed congressional staff, workers in both business and environmental lobbying organizations, and administrators in several Washington agencies. He found that business lobbies liked market incentives more than environmental lobbies, and Republicans liked them more than Democrats. He found that neither paid attention to efficiency considerations: those opposed to market incentives primarily wanted to avoid anything that legitimized any level of pollution, and those who favoured market incentives simply preferred the impersonal market to human regulators.

7.4 Winding Up

Eight years ago I was at a conference in Norway on the global environment and was interviewed for radio by a woman who asked me what Americans thought of 'green taxes.' I told her that I thought most Americans had never heard the term, but if they knew what it meant most environmentalists would be against green taxes. My response was mainly based on that survey of ten years earlier, and I believe now I was wrong in the answer I gave. For reasons I do not quite understand, the tide had turned in America and environmentalists were beginning to believe, as European environmentalists had already come to believe, that market incentives were often the superior mechanism.

In the same way, the notion that life is too precious to calculate its value is beginning to give way to the notion that resources devoted to human health and safety in the environment are limited, and should be focused on where they do the most good. But in many cases there will have to be changes in legislation to make it legitimate to prefer programs that can save many lives per million dollars spent to those that spend many million dollars to save a single life.

Economics is gradually penetrating the environmental community, but two decades was a long time to wait. Maybe during the interval economists spent too much time talking to each other and too little speaking clearly and simply in public.

PART III
ECONOMICS AND SOCIETY

8. The Proper Role of Theory

Edmond Malinvaud

This volume aims at improving communication between academic economists and policy makers, particularly on the difficult question of the relevance of economic research and education with respect to the problems of modern society. In this lecture I shall focus mainly on the role of theory in policy advising. But I shall also speak, at the beginning, about the place of theory in economic education and of research priorities for theory building (Section 8.1).

Policy advising, broadly understood, is where communication between academic economists and policy makers occurs. When considering it, we must have in mind that there are various conceptions about the content to be given to economic policy advising. Theory may play different roles, depending on the intended content (Section 8.2). This is why I shall discuss in turn two polar conceptions, which may be characterized under the labels of 'policy engineering' (Section 8.3) and 'providing principles for economic policy' (Section 8.4).

Theory must, of course, not be given here the narrow meaning it sometimes receives when it is identified with a mathematical model. Theory should rather be understood in the broad sense it should always have. A theory refers to a phenomenon or a problem and it provides a methodical intellectual construct, of a synthetic nature, for the knowledge and analysis of the phenomenon or problem. This construct is meant to be appropriate within a domain of some generality, subject to specified hypotheses. A science is made up of more or less tightly interrelated theories. With this broad definition, it makes no sense to set theory and empirical knowledge against each other: as soon as it claims to be valid beyond the data collected, empirical knowledge becomes theory; and any theory worthy of attention has an empirical base.

The title of this chapter suggests that, in economics nowadays, theory might not stand at its proper place. Indeed, the title echoes an often heard dissatisfaction of that sort. Where does the dissatisfaction come from? How could we improve upon the present state of affairs? The two questions will remain in the background of the following developments without being systematically repeated. In the conclusion I shall try to give my synthetic answers to them.

8.1   Economic Education and Research

Theories as vehicles of knowledge in teaching
With the definition given above, theories are natural vehicles for the transmission of scientific knowledge: presenting and explaining a theory is an efficient way of giving the result of a body of empirical knowledge and reflections. The theory summarizes this knowledge, usually based on many earlier investigations, and these reflections, usually elaborated through a process of trial and error. The summary so provided is intended to be sufficient for any application in the relevant domain, and so to make reference to earlier investigations and reflections then unnecessary.

It is therefore natural that teaching concentrates on theories, which of course should not be presented without explanation of their empirical and logical foundations, or without consideration of their actual domain of relevance. When theories bear on complex phenomena or are complex explanations of seemingly simple phenomena, they are embodied into mathematical models; this is done for accuracy and clarity. Teaching these models then is an efficient way of teaching theories, but does not exempt from verbal presentation of their content and justification.

However, there is a problem if the mathematical expertise of the students is too low to give them a good grasp of the best model of the theory, because if the model is exposed to them, theory is not really understood. The case is unfortunately frequent in economic teaching, with the result that models are often quoted out of place or misused by former students. The rule for the teacher faced with the problem should be to adapt the sophistication of his theoretical presentations to what students can best learn, even if he may then appear less knowledgeable than he really is. If we fear, as I do, that not all teachers are following this simple rule, we find a first reason for saying that economic education is 'too abstract'. But if there was no other reason, the argument would not go very far.

The main criticism is rather that teaching would give far too much attention to some phenomena and problems, and far too little attention to some other phenomena and problems. In particular the most abstract problems would be unduly stressed and the most pressing problems of modern society would be neglected. In other words, there would be a mismatch between the supply of knowledge to students and the demand of society with respect to what students ought to know.

Research and the progress of theories
But almost exactly the same criticism is addressed to academic economic research, following from the perception of a mismatch between the supply of new findings by research and the demand of society for new useful knowledge. This criticism deserves attention. Is it well-founded? If so, how can the mismatch be explained?

When we look back for progress in our discipline during the past four decades or so, we easily see important achievements concerning foundations and development of our theories. Given the nature of the criticism addressed to us, I shall just briefly quote improvements in the logical foundations and formalization of the main theories: we know much better now how to analyze uncertainties, information and interactive behaviour; the set of abstract models within which we can usefully put and answer a number of relevant questions is much richer and more fully explored. But I must insist more on research geared to empirical knowledge or to applications.

A lot of useful work was done on the forms of bounded rationality in individual behaviour, on the extent of substitutabilities in production, on the supply of labour and savings by households, on the impact of financial constraints, on patterns of evolution of prices in actual markets, with the importance of rigidities in the labour markets and that of speculative bubbles in financial markets. This work often is less conclusive than we had wished; but the fact is no reason for discarding the line of research.

Similarly, a good deal of attention was and is being spent on issues of direct interest to policy makers. Since I shall deal with these issues in the following sections, I may for the moment just point out in this respect environmental economics and a large part of macroeconomics, in which efficiency of various policy packages is directly at stake. For example no-one can deny the relevance of taking the formation of expectations into account in macroeconomics; no-one should either be surprised that it makes policy analysis less simple, to the point that it may turn out to be often inconclusive, given present knowledge.

But pleading in defence and showing what was achieved by economic research, as I just did, is not enough. We as economists have to recognize that satisfaction of demand is the acid test for evaluating the services provided by suppliers. Dissatisfaction on the demand side, with the perception of a mismatch, creates a problem for us as suppliers of knowledge. All the more so as the same perception is shared by many members of our profession, including some who greatly contributed to theoretical advance.

In science this type of mismatch is not uncommon. Research often tends to respond to inner concerns of the disciplines more than to outer requests. This is beneficial in the long run if, but only if, progress is so achieved, which will later permit to better meet the requests; unfortunately purely scholastic investigations may also prosper for long. Maybe the problem is more serious in economics than elsewhere. Some of our theoretical research may go much too far into discussing at length models of narrow relevance or problems very remote from significant results for the progress of knowledge.

One possible explanation of the mismatch should not be forgotten and probably has a good deal of truth. By its very nature, research does not always lead to new findings. In some areas significant findings are more difficult to reach than in others. Thus, what is published is not a good representation of the research efforts. Also, researchers may be reluctant to specialize on particularly difficult issues, for which success looks unlikely. For someone gifted in logics and mathematics, chances to produce publishable material are high if he or she concentrates on abstract theory, whereas many crucial empirical questions have so well resisted former attempts at answers that they offer gloomy prospects to young scientists.

This explanation goes a long way, because the demands of society to economic research are very difficult to meet. They concern complex phenomena; they request an easy cure of inflation, unemployment or high cost of credit. Actually, many of these demands are unlikely to be ever positively answered because they are asking for the unfeasible. But honest scientists often have to say that they do not know whether a question can receive a positive answer or not; so the frustration of demand goes on.

Proper incentives for research and teaching

We as economists have nevertheless to wonder whether the incentives for research in our discipline are not responsible for deviations that could be avoided. My feeling is that indeed this is the case. In particular I believe that reward goes too much now to mathematical skill. Notice that I do not want to play down mathematical economics as such; it is indispensable in the theory of a complex world. Notice also that the rewards were not the same fifty years ago, when mathematical economists were not so easily appointed in economics faculties or departments. But today too much praise is given to building and solving models of disputable relevance; too little is given to good pieces of economics as long as they contain no mathematical model.

On the teaching side the problem is a bit different. An economic education nowadays must give a mathematical background to students who would otherwise be lacking in it. But when learning economics proper, students should always be led to consider mathematics as a tool, not as an end in itself. This is why I insisted at the beginning of this section on the need to adapt teaching to the mathematical expertise of students. I also explained why some models are naturally used as supports in the teaching of theories. I concluded that, above all, the main question was to know whether the proper combination of theories, with their domains of relevance and their applications, was being taught.

Here again I believe there is a deviation, which may be explained by the reward system. Teaching pays too much attention to fads and fashions in economic research; a larger distance from current research would lead not only to more balanced programmes, but also to less importance being given to the formalism used in this research. Too often, however, professors of economics are appointed and promoted with reference to one dominant criterion: their contributions to current research, these contributions being judged mainly by the originality or sophistication of the models they exhibit.

8.2   Conceptions about Policy Advising

Advising political authorities and voters was an important motivation for many of those who built economic science. Any history of economics gives some room to the presentation of views held by renown scientists about economic systems and policies. Development of economic theories often went hand in hand with the expression of economic doctrines.

From the late 19th century at least, it became more and more frequent to see some ministers in charge of economy and finance being assisted by economic advisers. But the function and influence of these advisers varied, certainly for many reasons, but in particular because of shifts in the government economic doctrine.

Looking far back into the past would be out of place here. However, there is nowadays some uncertainty about what is the exact function of policy advising. Thus, it will be helpful to briefly consider in this talk how the dominant views changed since the middle of this century.

The story begins, of course, with Keynes, who was concerned with economic policy all along his life. His analysis recommended frequent interventions based on the state of business activity and expectations, using the tools of budgetary and monetary policies. His conception was shared by an increasing number of economists and politicians during the 1930s, but it was only in the fifties that it spread over practically all Western countries.

Keynes' ideas were subtle and flexible in many respects. Postwar Keynesianism was essentially simpler and clearer. Its conception of economic policy fitted well with that of a group of econometricians, whose most representative personality was Jan Tinbergen, soon followed by Lawrence Klein. The conception was presented in Tinbergen's books about economic policy; it stressed the functional relationship between policy instruments and objectives; it viewed advisers as 'policy engineers'. It was made systematic with the use of the macroeconometric models, which had been first introduced by

Tinbergen and his Dutch students, but were more widely promoted by Klein.

In the 1970s confidence in this conception was shaken, as macroeconomic policies were no longer seen as performing well in the medium run, while criticism was addressed to Keneysian theory and, still more, to the use of macroeconometric models for policy determination. Economic liberalism regained its earlier prestige, with the consequences that, in a number of countries, public firms were privatized and the announced intention was to discard macroeconomic policy activism in favour of a competition policy that stressed market flexibility.

In those countries, the conception about the part played by policy advisers went back to the one that was most often held at the beginning of the century. Economists called to serve as advisers in the older days were seen as experts in the rules of the market economy; they were guardians of economic orthodoxy; they were supposed to watch politicians and to protect them against their inclination to interfer in the markets; advisers had to exhibit to politicians the damaging long-run effects that would result from interventions; advisers had also to propose ways for dismantling institutions responsible for market rigidities and rent-seeking behaviour. Looking for a short label to be opposed to that of 'policy engineers', I may select here 'guardians of sound principles', it being understood that the so-called sound principles refer to the views of those holding the corresponding conception, not to principles that would be unanimously recognized as sound.

I do not think that this alternative conception is widely held as such now. We rather see a mixture of it with Tinbergen's one. Economic advisers have at times to act as policy engineers, at other times as guardians of the market mechanism and as enemies of protections and vested interests. From Tinbergen's conception they keep the idea that advisers do not choose the aims assigned to policies, but that they are competent to determine the policy package that would best reach these aims. With Tinbergen they are ready to be involved in the details of policy making and they know they must figure out, in quantitative terms, the effects of alternative policy packages. With the critics of Keynesian policy activism, they pay attention to medium- and long-run effects, in particular through favourable or detrimental effects on expectations and market incentives; they know that economists cannot be very accurate in practice and should refrain from taking sides when conclusions are not clearly determined.

In order to survey the role of theory in economic policy advising, it is convenient to look in turn at the two polar conceptions, because they lead to distinct considerations, which do not fundamentally conflict with each other and are most clearly seen in as simple a context as possible. This is why the two following sections will respectively be devoted to the role of theory in policy engineering and to its role in finding truly sound principles for policies.

8.3   Economic Theory for Policy Engineering

According to the policy engineering conception, advisers have to estimate and announce the effects of contemplated decisions to be taken by government. Estimation requires a model correctly tracing the relationship between variations in instruments of contemplated decisions and variations in the variables which are the targets. In most cases a purely qualitative model will not suffice to estimate even simply the direction of effects; so, most often a quantitative model is needed. Since pure theory will usually not give more than a qualitative model, values must be empirically found for a number of parameters. From our present point of view it does not matter much whether the relevant data are econometrically processed within the qualitative theoretical model, or whether the model is 'calibrated' by reference to parameter values which are, or were, otherwise estimated.

This conception is faced by two main challenges. In the first place, the economist has to correctly identify the origins of important indirect effects. Usually politicians think only in terms of direct effects, at which decisions are aiming. It certainly belongs to the economist to measure such effects, as precisely as possible, all the more so as politicians often tend to over-estimate them. But the economist has also to point to indirect effects, which may run counter or be damaging for other valuable objectives. Identification and measure of significant indirect effects is essentially more difficult than measure of direct ones.

The second challenge, by which I shall begin, concerns measurement within a supposedly correct model. A high degree of accuracy is fortunately not requested in practice. But rough orders of magnitude ought to be given. Unfortunately even that is difficult, given present econometric knowledge. Lack of accuracy in estimates of a number of elasticities is the problem: elasticities of the labour supply with respect to the wage rate, the unemployment rate, the generosity of unemployment benefit, ...; elasticities of household saving to the interest rate, to changes in income and wealth, ...; elasticity of labour productivity to changes in output and to capital intensity; and so on. Surveys show that, in each case, knowledge is hazy.

The problem is real and directly concerns economic theory, broadly defined as here. There is no easy cure and no alternative route, other than the one followed during the last decades. More extensive collection of data and more intensive processing of them will progressively lead to more accurate knowledge. All those concerned with efficiency of economic policies should support applied econometric research, the outcome of which is an asset, painfully accumulated but real.

The problem comes, at least in part, from the complexity of economic phenomena. The relevant elasticities involve partial derivatives and are not precisely defined unless one gives in each case the exact list of variables assumed to be held constant in estimation of each elasticity. Authors of surveys have the difficult but essential task of carefully distinguishing different definitions used in different econometric studies concerning the same broad behaviour, such as labour supply.

Difficulty in estimating important parameters was not enough taken into account in the older teaching about economic policy, particularly in the traditional methodology of macroeconometric models. It was assumed that, for policy analysis in a country, the best estimates of the relevant elasticities would be found by a fit of the macroeconometric model on past time series, in this country, of the aggregate variables present in the model. The methodology has to recognize that information about the values of parameters involves a much larger body of evidence than that given by the time series in question. Notwithstanding a serious risk of subjectivity or sloppiness in its application, the principle of some form of 'calibration' on the basis of external evidence has to be explicitly admitted and studied.

Even abstract theory, starting from agreed facts about economic structures and determinants of behaviour, has a part to play in the effort for improving the empirical knowledge required for policy advising. Indeed, this theory can provide new and better models within which econometric estimation will proceed.

A fortiori abstract theory is the unavoidable reference for the identification of indirect effects of decisions, the first challenge to the conception of policy advising that is now discussed. Dwelling upon the idea is not necessary, since economic education well conveys the conviction that interdependences explain indirect effects and are best analysed within a theoretical framework.

The question is just to know in each case which theoretical framework is reliable. It may be the Walrasian system with a simple addition of government, particularly when some long-term policy decisions are considered. But different systems will often be required: the monopolistic aspect of competition may be important; or the rigidity of wages and prices may matter; or liquidity constraints may be significant, particularly in the case of debt deflation; or a policy decision may change expectations; and so on. Clearly dogmatism is a danger, since it may lead us to uncritically accept out of place a preferred theoretical framework. Theoretical research, which gives a deeper understanding of theories, should be a protection against dogmatism, at least for those who do not take the latest fad in academic circles as providing the best representation of the world. In any case, almost all those who have been long involved in policy advising, and are sincere, must recognize that their explicit or implicit theoretical references have been eclectic. Such an attitude is correct, given the state of economic science.

8.4   Economic Theory and Sound Principles for Policy

The shift in the conception of policy advising and the return to the earlier one was obvious at OECD, where confidence in policy engineering was predominant around 1970, but has been much reduced since then. The recent *Jobs Study* (OECD 1995) in particular mainly insists on flexibility as a condition for efficiency of labour markets, and of economies more generally (some of the supporting material, however, contain estimates of effects). This is representative of a widespread change: the analysis of effects of decision, no matter how sophisticated it may become, is considered with suspicion. It is moreover viewed as very incomplete, because policy decisions are now regarded as interfering, positively or negatively, with conditions required for a good performance of market economies. Advocated conditions concern the nature and strength of competition, as well as the degree of mobility and flexibility; they may also concern removal of limitations to private initiative and private ownership; they may require a wishfully small size of government, and so on.

Looking for a proper theory of the world

This shift has a theoretical background and leads to a renewed role of theory. Precisely discussing the various theoretical aspects of the new conception, starting with its theory of the real economy, would clearly fall within the subject of this lecture, if that could be done fairly quickly. But such is not the case; the fundamentals are not made explicit; any attempt at doing so will show that not all proponents would give the same definition of these fundamentals.

Few, if any, would go as far as saying that the Walrasian competitive equilibrium provides the perfect reference to the real world for the purpose and that economic policy should aim only at implementing the conditions required for this equilibrium. This is so even though, on the surface, it seems that the hinted conditions for good performance of market economies refer to Walrasian theory. Actually, when economists approach particular policy issues they usually eschew competitive equilibrium language and speak in much more *ad hoc* terms, referring to a different world from that of any modern formal theory. In other words, whereas it is easy to point to weaknesses in the theoretical underpinnings of the policy engineering approach, it is much more delicate to present undisputable underpinnings of the new view, with respect both to the real world and to the policy prescriptions which are claimed to be appropriate.

The first task in a theoretical agenda about the subject ought to be an attempt at defining at least one benchmark theory that would provide an acceptable rationalization of the now most common policy prescriptions. I did not carry out this task and I am probably not best placed for doing so, since as a young economist I grew up within the policy engineering movement. I cannot do better here than explaining how I perceive the terms of the present challenge to both economic theory and policy advising, hoping that others will take as a research project to meet the challenge. Before building the wanted benchmark theory one will have first to survey again how the new conception emerged from experience, reflections and theoretical developments, then to sort out what opens new positive avenues to principles for economic policy, from what served only for a criticism of the older conception.

Limiting my theoretical ambition here to a lower level, I shall rather start from proximate explanations of the prevailing shift in the vision of policy advising and briefly reflect on their main consequences. According to me, the shift is explained by both a new concern for the longer-term implications of current policies and by more sophistication in the analysis of policy making. Let us look in turn at each one of these two reasons, before we try to assess, again but in this new perspective, what can be expected by policy makers from their economic advisers and from academic research.

Longer-term objectives of policies

Macroeconomic difficulties of the last twenty years compelled policy-makers and their advisers to pay more attention to the medium and long runs, than they did at the time of Keynesian fine-tuning. It was then realized that most macroeconomic models used in policy analysis were ill-suited for the study of other horizons than the short one. These models often did not even agree with the then-accepted 'neoclassical synthesis', according to which the proper guide for understanding phenomena was Keynesian or Walrasian theory, depending on whether they were short- or long-run phenomena.

The reaction was precisely to require from macroeconometric models, or more generally from all models used in policy analysis, that their implied long-run relations be consistent with a satisfory theory of the long run. Most often the latter theory had neo-classical foundations. The requirement imposed consideration of effects on assets, particularly on public debt. In the econometric methodology, on which we do not have to insist here, this requirement was often translated into the recommendation that behavioural equations be specified as meaning error corrections toward the respective rational long-run behaviours.

In macroeconomics the concern for longer-term effects was also associated with a revision of the diagnosis and underlying theory. At the turn of the 1980s in Western Europe, it appeared that deterioration in business profitability was still a more serious problem than lack of aggregate demand. Keynesian analysis, as it had been taught in the post war period, no longer looked fully appropriate; recognition of classical unemployment required that, in macroeconomic policy analysis, attention be given not only to aggregate demand and to short-run adaptations of prices and wages, but also to supply conditions. New specifications for econometric models were proposed in this spirit.

Concerns for the long term widened as it appeared that the European welfare state, which had been progressively built throughout earlier decades, was facing mounting problems. This was not only because of high unemployment, increasing costs of health services and prospective disequilibria of pension schemes faced to unfavorable demographic trends, but also because of what was called by Lindbeck (1995) 'hazardous dynamics' of the whole system: slowly but persistently existence of the system was inducing perverse changes in behaviours. Structural policies were then perceived by many as more important than macroeconomic policies. It was often thought that no deep analysis was required before concluding that some of these structural policies had to re-establish competition, market flexibility and market sanctions.

Developments in the theory of economic policy
The logic of policy intervention in modern market economies was also re-examined, starting from the so-called 'Lucas critique', or the so-called 'Ricardian equivalence', or still the so-called 'public choice theory'. On the whole, this re-examination was quite useful, notwithstanding errors in frequently premature conclusions that were too hastily drawn. Taking into account the time dimension, the effects of policies on expectations, the fact that governments could do and later undo for temporary political reasons (hence the role of credibility of announced policies), all that was quite to the point. It is

impossible to summarize in a few simple sentences the results of this re-examination, and this is precisely part of the problem we are now facing.

Policy analysis is bound to be very difficult if it has to rest on a reliable knowledge of both short- and long-term phenomena, with their interplay, and if it has to be couched in a complex logic, which involves many considerations, some belonging to political science.

Faced with this difficulty some draw the conclusion that government should not intervene, except in order to implement something like perfect competition with a balanced public budget, a neutral system of taxes and a strict monetary rule. The function of policy analysis would then be minimal. This position held by some economists, is obviously a 'non sequitur'. As long as this 'laisser faire' is not proved to be superior to any other form of government control and as long as the constituency will require some other form, policy analysis will have to be more sophisticated.

Indeed, sophistication follows from the realization that we cannot either just stand by our older practice neglecting the logical difficulties to which economic policy making may be exposed. After a proper economic analysis of the case, we still have to check and explain that our advice, inspired by this analysis, holds good notwithstanding these difficulties.

Some guidelines

What ought now to be expected by policy makers from their economic advisers and from academic research? In order to give an answer to the question, I shall begin by stating four recommendations to economists serving in government; I shall then briefly argue that many academic research lines are potentially relevant to economic policy making.

First recommendation: let economic advisers do the economics and political advisers do the politics. In the past decades it often happened that some economists approached political science (with the theory of social choices in the fifties, with public choice theory in the 1970s, with political economy now). A good deal of that research, which otherwise helped to bridge the gap between the disciplines, was and is relevant for economics. But it does not transform good economists into good political advisers: the subject is too narrow or the political side of the analysis is too simple-minded. Ministers have political advisers, with which economic advisers must certainly communicate for mutual understanding. But there is a natural division of roles. It then belongs to economists to worry mainly about the economic efficiency of the outcome of policies, indirect effects included, because others tend to neglect this efficiency, pressed as they are by interest groups and short-term considerations.[1] The main focus of academic research geared to policy advising should likewise be problems of macroeconomic and microeconomic efficiency.

Second recommendation: pay much attention to a correct diagnosis of the case. Indeed, policies are meant to serve given objectives within a given context. If the context is not well diagnosed, the policy has a good chance to miss its objective. Just to quote examples taken out of my experience as a macroeconomist, I recall that distinct diagnoses recommending distinct policy lines should have been made in my country in 1981 and in late 1992, stress being placed on the depression of business profitability in the first case, on debt deflation in the second. In our imperfect discipline different contexts often require different analytical frameworks; we must be open to eclecticism, as I already mentioned at the end of Section 8.3; we must be careful not to rely on an inadequate analytical instrument, which just happens to be available (too often did I see a macroeconometric model being used for evaluating a structural policy, whereas the model was obviously ill-suited for the purpose).

Third recommendation: improve and diversify the kit of instruments. This piece of advice naturally follows from what we just saw, but must also be made precise with respect to the once fashionable macroeconometric models, with which I begin. Clearly, the role of these models was overestimated twenty years ago, as well as the benefits to be drawn from even bigger models, which were also more costly to build and to use; I do not insist on the point. I must on the contrary warn against scrapping all such models and fully giving up the methodology introduced by Jan Tinbergen 60 years ago. The fact is that we have no alternative more reliable methodology, not only for macroeconomic policy engineering but even for good prospective assessments of business trends. Some such models must be kept up and even improved by a better inclusion of indicators of expectations and confidence in public policies. Other kinds of instruments should be developed, in particular microeconomic simulation models for evaluating the impacts of reforms of the welfare state, as well as analytical tools appropriate to feed cost-benefit analyses for microeconomic public decisions in various fields (public infrastructures, environment policies, and so on).

Fourth recommendation: be aware of the limits of scientific economic knowledge. Economic advisers should certainly go as far as they can in objectively analyzing the results to be expected from contemplated policies. On the other hand, there are also cases, even may be on some important issues, in which they should honestly signal that no conclusion about what is likely to result can be provided, given the state of economic knowledge. The problem with such rules of behaviour comes from the fact that a serious gap is very likely to remain for long between firmly established knowledge on one side, and demand for knowledge with policy purposes on the other. Among academic economists serving as advisers some will have to go somewhat beyond the limit of established science, so as to close part of the gap. They will have to rely on still unproven heuristic arguments, or on bold extrapolations of established facts. Actually, the economics profession has a long practice of such scientifically loose behaviour. I am simply stating that it is not bad from learned experts, if it does not go far. But we must realize that the new conception of policy advising gives more room to such behaviour than did the older one. The risk of ideological bias must then be kept in mind, all the more so as we had occasion to witness its materialization. This risk indeed is the main one to which economists working for government are exposed. It is undisputable, as it always was, that academic research can and will lead to improvements in policy advising, which beyond knowledge *per se* is the main aim of our discipline. In particular with the conception now prevailing, many lines of research are becoming still more relevant. Section 8.4 drew attention to the need for a proper benchmark theory. After that major request, special attention must be given here to the new dimensions brought in by the shift in conception: the medium and the long run, agents' expectations, policy rules, relative performances of economic systems with alternative legal and regulatory structures, and so on. For these dimensions, still more than for others, the main challenge is a better knowledge of economic phenomena.

8.5 Conclusion

Dissatisfaction about economic science and its expression in economic theories should appear natural today. In the older days we had a rather simple-minded notion of the use of economics. We could then see with optimism the operational application of our discipline. Both the inner development of the science and the downturn in business trends have challenged this notion. But they replaced it by a much more ambitious demand for knowledge, a demand which we can hardly meet and compels modesty from us.

There is no fast way to fundamentally improve upon the present state of affairs. Slowly and painfully economic research should bring a better grasp of at least some of the issues that are now baffling policy makers. Such is the main conclusion we ought to draw. We ought to convey the message to our students, communicating to them a strong sense of their mission in society. Incidentally, we should also be wary of the dangers to which our academic profession is exposed: appeals of the star system, appeals of a claim to mimic practices and incentives that perform well in 'exact sciences', and finally appeals of ideologies.

Note

1.   This is one of the main lessons coming out of the symposium 'Fifty years of the Council of Economic Advisers', *Journal of Economic Perspectives*, Summer 1996.

9. The Policy-maker's Demand for Economic Analysis

L. Ad Geelhoed

In a sense the topic of this volume directly relates to one of the basic propositions of economics, that is: 'specialization pays'. Indeed, in order to achieve a higher level of knowledge we must specialize: the specialist by definition knows more about his topic. Given the natural limitations to human comprehension, specialization is the royal road to a larger stock of knowledge (cf. Stigler 1963). Specialization, however, carries a price tag. One aspect of specialization is that specialists in one field have great difficulty in understanding specialists in another field, even in a narrowly defined subject area such as economics.

Presently many policy makers (and even trained economists, I presume) have great difficulty in understanding the relevance of the larger part of the activity that is going on at economic faculties and economics departments. They consider much economic work to be merely *l'art pour l'art*. To some, Huxley's 1937 wisecrack would seem to describe the present state of economics: 'Specialized meaninglessness has come to be regarded, in certain circles, as a kind of hall mark of true science'.

If economics is what most economists do, to paraphrase Viner, then we should conclude from much scholarly activity that

- mathematics is more important than history;
- analytics is more important than application; and
- creativity and communication are the least important skills of economists.

Accordingly, policy makers and economic scientists have expressed their concerns with respect to the way economic researchers respond to the problems of modern society.

This does not mean that economics has no large role to play in economic policy making. On the contrary, applied, concrete economic research is a cornerstone of economic policy making in most OECD countries. Many a bookshelf is filled with reports on economic policy. The point is that academic economists have to a large extent specialized in the production of sophisticated knowledge that has little relation to actual policy problems: it has become a less valuable asset to society.

9.1 The New Academic Role Model

One of the reasons for the current dichotomy between economic policy and economic theory is the increasing domination of a new role model of economic research that emerged somewhere in the mid-1980s. Essentially, the comparative advantage of the typical academic economist presently appears to lie in specializing in highly mathematical analyses that excel in rigour but not in applicability to current real world problems. The institutional context, or characteristics of the local economy, is generally not, or insufficiently, dealt with (see Frey and Eichenberger 1992, 1993, and Chapter 2 of this volume).

From a policy maker's perspective this globalization of economic research is worrying. The lack of a clear understanding of the institutional context and of the characteristics of the national economy is a deterioration. The aridity of economic science means that there is a permanent and increasing need for translation of its findings and for assessments of its relevance.

In the past this task used to be performed by university staff. However, since most economics professors want to publish in the leading American journals, empirical assessments and translation with a keen eye on the local (or European) context no longer seem to pay in academic circles. Consider Table 9.1 that is based on the so-called 'polderparade', an analysis of citations in the Dutch economic discourses.

Table 9.1   Ranking of Dutch Economists According to Quotations in the Dutch Economic Discourses (1993-1995)

Rank	Name	Principal affiliation	Number of quotations
1	A.L. Bovenberg	Central Planning Bureau	44
2	P.A.G. van Bergeijk	Ministry of Economic Affairs	42
3	M.M.G. Fase	DNB (Central Bank)	38
4	F.A.G. den Butter	Vrije Universiteit	33
5	C.A. de Kam	Groningen University	29
6	E.J. Bomhoff	Nijenrode Economic Forum	28
	J.J.M. Kremers	Ministry of Finance	28
8	J. van Sinderen	Ministry of Economic Affairs	27
9	H.W. de Jong	Emeritus Professor	26
	G.M.M. Gelauff	Central Planning Bureau	26
	A.H. Kleinknecht	Vrije Universiteit	26
12	J.J.M. Theeuwes	Leyden University	24
13	J.J. Graafland	Central Planning Bureau	22
	J. Hartog	University of Amsterdam	22
15	J.E. Andriessen	ING-Bank	21
16	L.A. Geelhoed	Ministry of Economic Affairs	20
	B. Nooteboom	Groningen University	20
18	F. van der Ploeg	Member of Parliament	19
19	B.M.S. van Praag	University of Amsterdam	18
	C.N. Teulings	Ministry of Social Affairs	18
21	D. Jacobs	TNO-STB Consultancy	17
	J.C. van Ours	Vrije Universiteit	17
23	J.A. Bikker	DNB (Central Bank)	16
	J. Pen	Emiritus professor	16
	A.R. Thurik	EIM (Institute Small Businesses)	16
	G. Zalm	Minister of Finance	16
27	W.H. Buiter	University of Amsterdam	15
	L. van der Geest	Nijenrode Economic Forum	15
	W. Groot	Leyden University	15
	S.K. Kuipers	Groningen University	15
	D.J. Wolfson	Scientific Council	15

The citation analysis covers four thousand quotations in the years 1993-1995 in six Dutch economic journals and the *Papers and Proceedings* of the Royal Netherlands Economics Association 'Koninklijke Vereniging voor de Staatshuishoudkunde'.[1] It offers some rough quantitative evidence for the 'Americanization' of the academic Dutch economic research industry: of this group of 31 economists that exert the strongest influence on the economic discussion in the Netherlands only 12 have their principal affiliation at a university (incidentally 10 earn a place in the Dutch ranking on the basis of international citations).

Thus Table 9.1 illustrates that most of the translation and application is being taken care of by policy makers at the ministries and the Central Bank and by researchers at the Central Planning Bureau. Indeed, academic economists do not meet this particular facet of society's demand for economic knowledge.

9.2   The Education of Economists

This neglect of reality and the down-playing of real world demands is even more problematic if one considers the position of education *vis-à-vis* research. Indeed, whereas 90 per cent of our students do not want to become scientists, both graduate and post graduate education in economics still appears to aim at providing the foundation for a scientific career.[2] In 1994, the American Carnegie foundation for the advancement of teaching published a study that provided an international perspective on the academic profession (Boyer et al. 1994). This investigation shows that Dutch university staff consider research much more important than teaching. Whereas commitment to teaching predominates in American countries and Russia, Dutch academic interest strongly leans to research. In this respect the Netherlands is also well ahead of Japan, Sweden and Germany (Boyer et al. 1994, Figure 15).

A gap between economic theory and policy oriented research is evident in the 1996 report by the 'Review Committee of Economic Science in the Netherlands' (Lubbers Committee 1996) that signals different 'conversational subcultures' that are also reflected in economic education. These problems are not typically Dutch as shown by several inquiries by committees of the American Economic

Association on the education and training of graduates and economic doctorates in the US (Hansen 1991).

I argue that our society will be worse off if its students are trained to solve the problems of the US economy. As you are probably aware, the Netherlands is an overtaxed economy with low inflation, a current account which is persistently in surplus and a dramatically high share of long-term unemployed. This makes it surprising to see that graduate teaching in the Netherlands focuses on the US problems of high inflation, a current account deficit and strong fluctuations in unemployment (around a much lower trend level than in Europe). According to the 1996-1997 course programmes of the University of Amsterdam, Groningen University, Maastricht University, Tilburg University and the Vrije Universiteit Amsterdam, students will have to read N.G. Mankiw's *Macroeconomics* as the main text in their first year.[3] At Erasmus University Rotterdam the main text is R.J. Gordon's *Macroeconomics*.

All in all economic students start their first year with an introductory textbook that puts the American economic issues on the front row. Many of these students are motivated by the problems of Dutch society. They either have to become disappointed or to adjust and to internalize the implicit message to consider these problems of minor importance for mastering their subject field. Here, in my opinion, European economists (especially in the Netherlands) should listen to American advice as put forward by Krueger et al. (1991, p. 1052). They argue that educational programmes should pay 'sufficient attention to applications and real-world linkages to encourage students to start applying the concepts themselves' (see also Harberger 1993 on the importance of restructuring the curriculum so as to help to see the world more clearly).

The policy-maker's tool kit

When asked what I consider to be the most important elements of an economic policy maker's tool box, I always refer to Schumpeter's (1954) *History of Economic Analysis*, especially the second chapter that deals with the techniques of economic analysis. Schumpeter distinguished three fields:

- economic history;
- statistics;
- theory.

Interestingly, Schumpeter considers economic history to be the most important of these fundamental fields:

> If I were told that I could only study one of [these fields] but could have my choice, it would be economic history that I should choose. (Schumpeter 1954, p. 12)

I think Schumpeter is right where he argues that this is so because (i) a command of historical facts is necessary to understand economic phenomena; (ii) most of the fundamental errors in economic analysis relate to a lack of historical experience rather than to other shortcomings of the economist's tool box; and (iii) studying history is the best method to understand how economic and non-economic (institutional) 'facts *are* related to one another and how the various social sciences *should* be related to one another' (Schumpeter, 1954, p. 13 original emphasis).

Next comes a command of modern statistical methods that is 'a necessary (but not a sufficient) condition for preventing the modern economist from producing nonsense' (Schumpeter 1954, p. 14). I find it particularly disappointing that the quality and accuracy of economic observations are hardly dealt with by academic economists. The 1990 special issue of the *Economic Journal* on the state of economics in the next century did not include a syllable on statistics. This suggests that economists take the data for granted.

The third fundamental field is theory, the field that nowadays appears to be considered the most important by academic economists. Incidentally this is a field that is wrongfully and discomfortably often forgotten by policy-makers; it is the combination of the three fundamental fields in combination with integrity and writing and negotiating skills that constitute the human capital of a successful economic policy-maker.

To this list (economic history, statistics and theory), that is relevant for any economist whether he is a policy-maker or a scientist, I would add the following items that constitute especially relevant elements of the policy-maker's human capital stock:

- knowledge about society (incidentally, Schumpeter adds 'economic sociology' later in the *History*'s second chapter);
- knowledge about the international economic context; and
- knowledge about the possibilities and limitations of the policy instruments.

Comparatively speaking, Dutch students are trained in techniques rather than in relevant applications or economic history.[4] The consequence is that economic policy may be misdirected unless we retrain those students that want to work in the private sector or become policy-makers in the public sector.

Actually this is what we are doing in the Netherlands, as the ministries of Economic Affairs, Finance, Foreign Affairs, Social Affairs and Transport and Public works and Water management finance a graduate trainee programme for policy-makers (BOFEB). This trainee programme is a success. Each year more than 200 students apply; the rejection rate is about 90 per cent.[5] The BOFEB hires high quality university staff and policy-makers to lecture in order to provide the trainees with a good working knowledge of how theoretical insights can be applied to the questions that Dutch policy-makers face. It is by no means accidental that many lecturers at this institute are on the shortlist of Table 9.1, as it contains the so-called 'gate keepers' that make the translation from science to policy.

The existence of the BOFEB obviously is not a consequence of the fact that universities provide general education, while employers have to provide 'on the job training' since this is an efficient division of labour that does not justify a training facility. The reason why the BOFEB was created is that many economists at Dutch universities no longer seem to consider the characteristics of their country as part of the general education they provide: the teaching of economics has become 'footloose'.

In this sense the present trend in economic analysis and education seems to reflect a choice for 'high tech economics' rather than for 'human capital'. All in all, this leaves us with an astonishing paradox. Economic science is founded on the premises of optimality and rationality, but is unable or unwilling to apply these principles on itself, leaving the market for economic knowledge in constant disequilibrium.

9.3 Why the Gap Needs to Be Bridged

Can economics be characterized as a science that is looking for a market? I will argue that the interaction between policy and research will,

- first, provide economic science with such a market; and
- second, that this interaction will provide interesting questions and inspiration that will stimulate economic science.

In doing so, I will first take a short look at the history of economic science. Next I will deal with a set of interrelated questions that derive from the observation that economics as social science needs to take topics into account that have a relevance for society.

The founding fathers of economic science, as you are probably well aware, were involved in *political* economy. The discussion in this volume would have astonished them. Economic policy and economic science were considered to be two sides of the same coin. For example, Adam Smith was the first to point out the benefits of the division of labour. Apparently, however, he did consider it natural to deal with theory and policy at the same time. Indeed, Smith would most probably not have considered the present division between economic science and economic policy as the logical result of the economic principle of specialization. On the contrary, in the *Wealth of Nations* Smith (1776, p. 318) argues that science is the great antidote to the poison of enthusiasm and superstition. Accordingly, Smith proposes that candidates for public offices should undergo an examination in the higher and more difficult sciences. Clearly then, Smith considers scientific knowledge to be an essential asset for policy-makers.

Next consider Marshall. It is customary to consider Marshall's *Principles of Economics* as a point of demarcation (although before Marshall many authors emphasized the autonomy of economics as a science). Marshall dropped the adjective political from the title of his main work: it is not the *Principles of Political Economy*, but the *Principles of Economics*. Marshall, moreover, argues that economics avoids

> many political issues, which the practical man cannot ignore: and it is therefore a science, pure and applied, rather than a science and an art. And it is better described by the broad term Economics than by the narrower term Political Economy. (Marshall ([1890]1920, p. 43)

Marshall's orientation, however, is always practical from the start and he argues in the *Principles* that the dominant aim of economics is to contribute to a solution of social problems. Marshall states that economics should aim at helping the statesman to determine not only what the ends of economic policy should be, but also what the best instruments are of a broad policy devoted to those ends.

Allow me to jump one century and focus on the contemporary message of this argument. It is the confrontation of theory and reality that is the cornerstone both of empirical economics and of economic policy-making. It is important to understand that economics is a social science that ultimately aims at providing rational foundations for decisions in economic policy-making at the microeconomic, mesoeconomic and macroeconomic level.

This interaction between policy and science benefits economists along two channels. First, any economic policy-maker that does not take scientific analyses into account risks being guided by essentialist premises with a high ideological content. Obviously this is a very grave loss for society. Second, economic science that does not want to consider policy relevance (in a very broad sense) as one of the touchstones of what is good science will ultimately lose sight of its purpose as a *social* science. Economic science can only set the agenda for the economic and the public discours if it considers topics that are relevant for policy-makers. This is the lesson of the life and work of such outstanding economists as Keynes and Tinbergen.

9.4　Economics from the Island

Presently, economic science often appears to make behavioural analyses of constructed worlds rather than of the observable reality.

This movement from observation to construction increases the danger that economists get stuck on an island. Interestingly, as you are probably well aware, many jokes exist about economists that get stuck on an island. The joke is that they solve the day-to-day problems of Robinson Crusoe by assumption: 'It's simple ... Assume you have a tin opener ... Assume you have a hammer, etcetera'. My point is that by betting all one's money on Assumption, Hypothesis and Logic, economists will ultimately isolate themselves from policy-makers and will be unable to play a meaningful role in the public debate. Theory is necessary for any advancement (also in applied and policy oriented research), but to rely only on theory enhances the danger of producing irrelevant or simply silly results.

The transition of Eastern Europe

Let me give an example. At the outset of the 1990s an important policy question was how we could best assist the transformation of the formerly Centrally Planned Economies 'from Marx to market'. The Centre of Economic Policy Research (Begg et al., 1990) provided a timely report in which it estimated the required annual capital flow to Central Europe on the basis of a target growth rate for per capita income (a doubling in ten years time), a constant capital-output ratio and an assessment of the quality and quantity of the available factors of production. It contains amongst its 'policy relevant' conclusions an assessment that the West should annually provide $135-$291 billion in aid to Central Europe.

The logic of the conclusion cannot be disputed: given the assumptions and the growth target, this sum of money is the result of the calculations. The relevance of the advice, however, was considered doubtful from the start by our economic departments, because the CEPR's estimates would represent an unrealistically high share in the recipient's GDP (of about a quarter to a half) and it was questioned whether these amounts could actually be absorbed at all.

Indeed, calculations at the Netherlands Ministry of Economic Affairs showed that an export-oriented growth strategy might equally well provide the necessary funds for the transition (Oldersma and van Bergeijk 1992). A more detailed analysis revealed that the CEPR proposal would actually result in a substantial excess of consumption growth over GDP growth, a reduction in savings ratios and a marked loss in average capital productivity so that the CEPR's stated target of doubling Central Europe's per capita GDP in ten years could not be achieved by its proposed massive injection of concessional capital (van Bergeijk and Lensink 1993). Fortunately, European policy-makers did not follow the CEPR's logic and the policy analyses that actually shaped European policies towards Eastern Europe were driven by relevance.

9.4 Science and Policy

Science often complains that politics does not listen, that politics is not interested in science, that politics needs science only to support its ideology. For this reason many scientists turn their back on politics. It is, however, no solution to opt out. If science is a bad salesman, then science is also to blame if policy is ideologized. Again this suggests that the interaction between science and policy should be more intense.

Fortunately, like Europe (where the internal market and EMU are grounded on piles of high quality research) the Netherlands has a rather rational approach to policy-making. The Dutch approach has been inspired by the work of Tinbergen. Generally speaking, this approach prevents selective pickings and ideological economic policies such as Reaganomics and Thatcherism. In the Netherlands, economic science provides both theories and concepts that influence the public debate on economic and social policies. Moreover, scientific work gives policy-makers useful analytical frameworks that can help them to analyse considered policy alternatives from many points of view. This analysis from many angles, so to say, may provide us with a better understanding of the robustness of policy prescriptions. In this sense, science is a cornerstone of policy and enriches the operational debate on policy.

Science provides an important justification for many policies. Indeed society has grown much more assertive. Government organizations are constantly being interrogated about the rationale of their actions. Essentially, government agencies have three justifications:

- they implement parlementary/democratic decisions;
- they behave in accordance with constitutional demands; and/or
- their acts are guided by an analysis of the comparative efficacy and efficiency of alternative policies that aim at comparable goals.

The ultimate justification obviously is the third one; namely whether policies are effective and efficient. Indeed, even a proposal that is supported by two thirds of parliament will ultimately become unacceptable if it does not show success. This is the rationale for the policy-maker's interest in the achievements of economic science. The more scientifically based policy-making becomes, the stronger the interaction between economics as a science and the art of economic policy needs to be.

The art of economics

This is not to say that policy-makers should sit and wait until academics have done their job. On the contrary, while the logical order of things suggests that logic supersedes the art of policy-making, the historical order is often the other way round:

> The reason is that the demand for guidance arising from men's practical needs is recognised, and attempts are made to satisfy it, before bodies of speculative truth are systematically formulated. ... But, as we have said, in the logical order science precedes art, for we cannot satisfactorily lay down rules for practical guidance except on the basis of knowledge of facts. When, therefore, this knowledge is not found elsewhere, the art must seek it as best it can for itself, thus becoming at the same time both a science and an art, the two enquiries, however, not being definitely distinguished. Strictly speaking, instead of saying that historically art precedes science, it would ... be more accurate to say that at the outset there is no clearly marked line of distinction between them. (J.N. Keynes, 1891, pp 39-40, footnote 1)

Indeed, many Dutch policy-makers have produced high quality scientific knowledge over the last couple of years. Knowledge that provides answers to new important economic questions related to, for example, the impact of taxation on the supply side of the economy, the costs and benefits of an ecotax, endogenous growth and the importance of technology policy and the macroeconomic consequences of privatization, deregulation and competition policy.

Academic economists are following up on these explorations as, for example, shown by the fact that since 1993 research with respect to competition has increased (van Gent 1997). In a sense academic scientists take over the baton from policy-makers. Indeed, economic science should not neglect its vocation to provide critical evaluations of the technical arguments.

According to some observers, a trend towards less ideologically determined policies is evident and they point for example towards the developments in the world economic system. Where the conflict between the major ideologies seems to have been resolved in favour of market oriented systems, one expects that rationality instead of ideology will become a more important ingredient of the public debate on policies. Economic science is especially relevant for this debate as its theories and methodologies help policy-makers to get a better grip on the effects and unintended side-effects of policies.

9.6   The Policy-maker's Demand

For the future, I think it is essential for economic science to keep an open mind to new developments, both in policy, and in science. New ideas should receive a fair chance. In the past, all too often new ideas were referred to as pies in the sky. Examples are the incorporation of the notions of supply siders in economic analyses, and the beneficial effects of a strengthening of market forces that once were considered to be 'unsubstantiated claims by ideologically inspired policy enterpreneurs', but which by now are part and parcel of mainstream economic analysis.

Policy-makers do not need to know everything. We do not need the perfectly logical analysis. We need guidance, and we need it now. We do not need so much light that every little corner of a problem can be investigated. We simply need sufficient and sufficiently reliable knowledge in order to prevent falling from the stairs or bumping against a blind wall. Indeed, if we can prevent the most serious policy errors, the policy generally speaking is not bad at all.

Fundamental policy questions

In this respect, it is alarming to see that the fundamental questions Western European policy-makers are confronted with - the questions of institutional change, the optimal social economic order and the accompanying transitional issues - have hardly been adressed by economic scientists. In the Netherlands, this may reflect risk aversion on the part of both the funders and the recipients of research grants for pure scientific research on these very difficult issues.[6] The apparent unwillingness to address fundamental policy questions may also be caused by a lack of competition as economists that do not work at a Dutch university cannot apply for the research grants. So it may be useful to redesign the funding of research shifting from an output commitment to an input commitment (that is, the amount of effort to be put into a difficult, risky research question) or to allow for international competition with respect to national scientific research budgets. The lack of fundamental research into fundamental policy questions may, however, also reflect the unwillingness of economists to look beyond the Economic Question. In this respect a caveat is in order. Lewin uncovers a 'pathological pattern' in the relationship of academic economists and scientists in other disciplines:

> It appears that throughout this century, economists have been reluctant to acknowledge the interdependence between economics and its sister disciplines, particularly sociology and psychology. Only under pressure will we acknowledge our dependence, and even then, our attention focuses almost exclusively on the psychological shortcomings of economics, rather than on the sociological shortcomings which are much more fundamental and difficult to address. (Lewin 1996, p. 1295)

Economics should drop the pretension that economic science can provide the ultimate and optimal policy prescription for the highly complex and highly dynamic system in which we happen to live. This calls for a multidisciplinary approach: economics may be the queen of the social sciences, but policy-makers should look beyond her speech from the throne. For this reason also, economics as a social science should stay in a penetrating contact with its context.

Economic science, art or asset? My answer is: Yes economic science is an asset. But it is an art to keep economic science in contact with society.

Notes

Robert Haffner skillfully assisted in the preparation of the manuscript.

1. The six journals are: *Economisch Statistische Berichten, De Economist, Financiële en Monetaire Studies, Maandschrift Economie, Openbare Uitgaven* and *Tijdschrift Politieke Ekonomie.*

2. Actually, according to a recent survey by Hulshof et al. (1996) only 52 per cent of Dutch economists that got their PhD since 1990 work at a university. Interestingly 32 per cent of these 'young' PhD's want to work in consultancy in the next 5 years.

3. The University of Amsterdam advises M. Bourda and C. Wyplosz, *Macroeconomics: A European Text* as secundary reading, but this is not a text for the formal examination.

4. Two references on this topic (in Dutch) are van der Ploeg (1992, pp. 92-3) and van Sinderen (1992). Not everybody is unhappy with the situation. See, for example, Kapteijn and de Zeeuw (1991).

5. Applicants have to pass through an intensive procedure that includes a series of inteviews. The first round of the procedure involves the writing of an essay on three topics that are relevant for policy making and a short test that investigates the applicant's knowledge of the Dutch economy. The test comprises questions such as 'What is the level of GDP?' or 'What is the long term interest rate?' About 75 per cent of the applicants fail at least 50 per cent of these simple questions about the Dutch economy although margins of error of 25 per cent are applied when assigning marks.

6. The Dutch procedure involves an assessment of the risk that the project will not yield the results that it is hoped to produce which is not an appropriate requirement for 'blue sky' research.

10.   Why Things are Different

The motivation for this book is the view that a lack of communication
between scientists and policy-makers hurts both science and policy.
On the one hand, there is the risk that economic theory becomes
detached from the real world and hence becomes irrelevant. On the
other hand, there is the danger that policy practitioners fall back on
pre-scientific ideas or ideologies if they are not confronted with
scientific insights. In short, lack of communication may produce
disinterested scientists and ignorant policy-makers. Accordingly, we
asked ourselves and the contributors the following questions:

- To what extent is communication between academic
  economists and policy practitioners lacking?
- Does the missing market for ideas have adverse consequences?
- If so, what inhibits the free flow of ideas and what measures
  should be taken to remove the barriers to trade?

As is common in economics, the answers are not straightforward;
rather they are of the type 'on the one hand ..., but on the other hand
...' One important reason why the conclusion cannot be simple is that
the market for economists is large with a lot of variety. It does not
make sense to throw all of economics on one heap. On the contrary,
as Adam Smith pointed out, specialism pays. So diversity is, or can
be, beneficial and economists should not be forced into the same
mould. This chapter aims to bring out several dimensions of the
problem, showing that while some arguments may be relevant for a
certain type of economics, they need not be relevant for all
economics.

10.1 Different Types of Irrelevance

There is a general impression with the public and even among
economists that economic science does not offer much help in

adressing the major economic problems of today. There is a perception of mismatch between the supply of new findings by scientific research and the demand for useful knowledge by society. Malinvaud, in his contribution, reminds us that such concerns are not unique to economics. In any science, one may hear the complaint that research activity is too far removed from practical concerns. Should we conclude that science is irrelevant? The answer to this question is a simple 'No'. It is a misunderstanding that a science can be judged by its ability to predict or to solve problems, certainly when problems are complex. Scientific activity is the systematic attempt to understand the world and a science should be judged by the insights that it yields. Of course, economics is especially vulnerable to the above criticism since the failures of economists are so clearly visible. Economic problems are percieved to be very important in modern society. Economists thus have ample opportunities to show how little they understand of how the economy works.

An important question is thus to what extent the irrelevance of economic science is only perceived and to what extent it is real. If it exists, what causes it and what can be done about it? Portes argues that the irrelevance is only perceived. Economic science yields important insights and provides answers to those questions for which answers can reasonably be expected. Portes argues that the problems posed to economists are very complex ones to which an immediate answer cannot always be provided. If an answer can be given, the answer is typically not simple. Policy-makers and the public at large, however, desire simple answers. The simplification of the original answers creates disagreements among economists: some economists stress one aspect, others another so that trade-offs vanish into the background. Portes is not concerned about the failing predictions of economists. Making predictions is not the core business of economists. Moreover, predictions may be wrong simply because the input was wrong or incomplete.

Jacquemin, discussing the relation between the theory of industrial organization and competition policy, illustrates the important point that scientific progress, leading to better insight, need not make life simpler for the policy-maker. For example, when science uncovers new trade-offs, the policy-maker may be tempted to consider the new insights to be irrelevant. The 'old' industrial organization literature was simple: theory postulated a linear relation between market structure, market conduct and market performance, while empirical work sought to relate performance and structure directly to each other. This simple framework turned out to be unsatisfactory: the empirical relations were weak and not robust and, theoretically, the linear relation was unjustified. This unsatisfactory state of affairs gave rise to a more sophisticated approach using game theory. It yielded a proliferation of models that all attempt to capture specific aspects of the complex interrelationships between structure, conduct and performance. One may regret the resulting fragmentation, but the proliferation of models may simply reflect the fact that the world is more complicated than was initially believed. Paradoxically,

> we may conclude that the models produced by the new Industrial Organization in this domain have improved the quality and the relevance of our analysis. Nevertheless, simultaneously, they have made the dilemma faced by the Antitrust Authorities more complex.

Schelling discusses three reasons for the irrelevance of economics, which all originate from the fact that many policy discussions are dominated by value judgments to which economists have little to contribute. The most extreme form that Schelling discusses is when the policy debate remains entirely ideological, when the decision makers (and/or the public) refuse to discuss the issue in a rational, scientific way. People may hold such strong convictions or beliefs that they may be unwilling to be persuaded by a scientific analysis. As Schelling remarks, it may be a rational strategy for a government official seeking reelection not to put a value-laden item on the agenda: 'The issue ... cannot even be raised in public by a senior government official without a resulting clamor for resignation'.

A second reason why economists may have little to contribute to the policy debate is that the economic arguments may simply be banned from the discussion. Schelling sees two main contributions of economic analysis to environmental policy: cost-benefit analysis and replacing direct regulation by market incentives. Yet

> environmental regulation ... is, or is perceived to be, about saving lives. Life and death are a subject that many people, including legislators and administrators, believe should not be contaminated by cost considerations.

A third reason is that economists themselves may be divided about their value judgments. Recall the distinction between positive economics (that aims at understanding and is essentially value free) and normative economics (that aims at providing policy advice and in which value judgments enter). According to Friedman

> differences about economic policy among disinterested citizens derive predominantly from different predictions about the economic consequences of taking action - differences that in principle can be eliminated by the progress of positive economics - rather than from fundamental differences in basic values ... about which men can ultimately only fight. (Friedman 1953, p. 5)

Friedman is thus optimistic that progress in economic science will lead to agreement on policy. Schelling's contribution, however, suggests that essential differences will remain, that even if understanding is increased, economic insights will not settle differences of opinion because they will not close the value gap.

This completes our overview of arguments why economics may not be as irrelevant as is sometimes thought and why economic science should not always be blamed for perceived irrelevance. This classification basically deals with the demand for economic knowledge. The next sections explore the supply side. Could economic science be even more relevant? If so, how could this be achieved?

10.2   Different Types of Economics

The spectrum of research activities that economists perform ranges between two extremes, from fundamental research to policy research In the interior of the spectrum falls 'applied' economics, which transforms the insights from fundamental research into principles that guide policy and applies the tools provided by a combination of science and statistics to address either problems uncovered by policy or puzzles turned up by the economic system. Boundaries are, of course, vague. Moreover, as Portes remarks, applied economics should not be equated with policy analysis: it is substantially broader. Portes also makes the value judgment that good economics involves both thorough knowledge of theory and sophisticated application.

If Portes' values were widely shared in the profession, praise should go to those who are able to successfully apply existing theory, not to those who develop theory, nor to those who implement the insights resulting from application. Malinvaud does not reveal his values but he suggests that, at present, researchers receive too little credit for good pieces of economic work:

> the reward goes too much now to mathematical skill ... too much praise is given to building and solving models of disputable relevance; too little is given to good pieces of economics as long a they contain no mathematical model.

In short, the incentives are wrong; they yield research, that, as Frey and Eichenberger argue, focuses more on rigour and formal elegance than on providing insights on how the economic system actually functions. Furthermore, Frey and Eichenberger are concerned that increased globalized competition and intensified competition will further strengthen the incentives to perform irrelevant research.

The problem of the wrong balance in economic research can be approached from three alternative angles. First, consider the tools that a scientific economist has at his disposal. Schumpeter (1954) distinguishes four fundamental fields: history, statistics, theory and economic sociology. Using modern terminology, we would say that a professional economist should have a good knowledge of the relevant economic institutions, of the data of the economy (as well as of the statistical methods used to compile these and the problems involved), of the historical evolution of these data and institutions, and of economic theory. Whereas economic theory supplies the tools of analysis, the other three fundamental fields supply the content material to which the tools can be applied.

The imbalance of research amounts to a criticism that there is excessive emphasis on theoretical refinement at the expense of the other fundamental 'techniques'. Hence emphasis is on improving the methods of analysis, rather than on content. As Geelhoed writes, academic economists have to a large extent specialized in

> highly mathematical analyses that excel in rigour but not in applicability to ... real world problems [and a] lack of a clear understanding of the institutional context and of the characteristics of the national economy is a deterioration.

Next, consider the activities of the scientific economist. In essence, scientific activity compromises three different stages:

- observation of the real world and construction of a simplified model that incorporates the essential elements of interest;
- deduction of the consequences of the model; and
- confrontation of these consequences with observed data.

Of these three stages, the second one is purely logical and mathematical. The first and the third stages - the creative construction of the model including the judgment involved in selecting the 'right' model - and the confrontation of the insights derived from the model with the real world, constitute the essence of economics. While the praise should go to those economists who excel at the first and/or third stages, it actually goes to those with mathematical skills. Consequently, too much emphasis is given to the second stage (the analysis of models of disputable relevance) and too little to the first and third stages.

Consider the markets on which the academic economist is active. The demand for his services arises from two sources: from his fellow scientists and from the policy-makers and the public who want to be enlightened on how the economic system functions. Critics argue that research efforts are too much directed to concerns that are purely internal to the science at the expense of efforts devoted to practical concerns. Economists are working on puzzles that they cooked up themselves, rather than on models and problems that are inspired by reality. Of course, such an argument applies to any science: as a science develops, it automatically generates intellectually challenging problems not directly related to practical issues and some scientists are motivated to try to solve these. Malinvaud argues that this may be beneficial in the long run. Nevertheless, he suggests that purely scholastic investigations may prosper for too long and that this problem may be especially serious in economics.

After having presented these different perspectives on the problem, we now turn to analysis. Why would economists specialize on the wrong tools and the wrong problems? Why would applied research be undervalued? Why are the incentives wrong?

Frey and Eichenberger locate the reason for the faulty incentives in the academic review process. They write:

> The quality of a professional contribution can only be evaluated with respect to internationally valid aspects. Formal rigour and elegance perfectly meets this requirement[, but] academic contributions based on an extensive knowledge of local conditions and institutions cannot be judged by an external scholar.

Frey and Eichenberger argue that aspects that are difficult to judge will not be judged, especially not in a situation where there are multiple referees who are not familiar with institutional settings. Accordingly, only technical aspects - rigour and formal elegance - are evaluated. Obviously, if evaluators do not pay attention to a certain aspect, then, given the incentive to publish, the researcher rationally chooses not to devote much attention to it. Hence, the overemphasis on formality and theory. In Frey and Eichenberger's view, a scientist is driven both by an intrinsic motivation to understand the world and by the incentives that the academic market provides. The latter incentives are strongly biased against relevant real world issues. According to Frey and Eichenberger, globalization and increased competition worsen the situation: in an international market it is less likely to meet a referee with knowledge of local conditions. Hence, the relevance of the model is even more difficult to judge and thus gets correspondingly less weight.

Whereas these arguments probably contain some truth, we doubt that it is the entire truth. If correct, there should be even less empirical and institutional content in research papers. The constant flow of heavily empirically oriented NBER working papers cannot be considered as trivial examples of elegance of technique. Indeed, one cannot accuse the 'stars' of the profession (winners of Nobel Prizes, the Bates Clark medal, and so on) of doing irrelevant work. Some of the very best people in the profession are also involved in empirically oriented work, suggesting that such work does bring substantial professional payoff. In fact, van Dalen and Klamer show that both Americans and Dutch graduates considerably appreciate economists who do applied work that sheds light on the real world. Perhaps a science should be judged on the basis of the best work that it produces. One has to accept that a large proportion of the research is irrelevant, because this is inherent in the business. In short, it does not seem to be the case that the profession does not value good applied work.

Given that empirical work is desirable and at the same time both labour and capital intensive, it seems worth the trouble to design new incentive structures that favour empirical work. European funding of research networks, teams of research workers that devote themselves to the same topic across Europe, could be an important stimulus in this respect. It is not only a matter of money. In particular peer-review systems can deliver more and better empirical studies only if referees take the importance of such work better into account.

10.3   Different Types of Theory

Theory is not always interpreted in the broad sense that Malinvaud rightly argues should be the case:

> Theory should ... be understood in the broad sense it should always have. A theory refers to a phenomenon or a problem and it provides a methodical intellectual construct, of a synthetic nature, for the knowledge and analysis of the phenomenon or problem.

The narrow meaning that equates theory to a mathematical model is used quite frequently. This may lead to sterile formal theorizing that could be rightly accused of being too far removed from the real world. At present, the two conceptions of theory exist side by side in economics. We labelled the extremes 'high tech economics' (that is, a sterile, formalistic non-contextual approach) and 'human capital economics' (high quality applied research that is transparently linked to the context of the real world).

Colander (1992) argues that economic theory should be allowed to stand by itself: one should not insist on direct policy relevance. If positive economics is freed from the constraint to be policy relevant, it might be more imaginative and ultimately more useful. Moreover, it frees applied economics from the perceived need to employ the methodology of positive economics. Solving problems is a different activity than testing theories. It involves judgment about which theory is most relevant and applying it while taking its limitations into account. A rigourous scientific procedure is not always necessary, nor desirable, to reach solutions to an actual problem. In the situation where the solution depends on the integration of solutions to various sub-problems, the results of an analysis can only be as exact as the least precise part of the analysis. Accordingly, there is no point in improving the exactness of just one part of the solution if the other parts remain very imprecise. In particular, if the facts are difficult to ascertain, using sophisticated technical econometric analysis to analyse these data may not make much sense.

One reason for the advancement of 'high tech theory' may have been the combination of extensive specialisation (within academia there are experts in every technique) and a lack of communication between the various experts. Why has so little trade occured between the specialists? Why did each cater only to his own specialized market? We discuss these questions in the next section. For now, we conclude that the different types of theory coexist, that there is room for both, but that one type may be more valuable than the other, and that the latter may be overrepresented at present.

10.4 Different Types of Economists

We have defined a professional economist as a person who masters certain 'techniques' (history, institutions, data, statistical methods, and theory) and who is supplying ideas and insights derived from these 'techniques' on various markets. We have distinguished between three markets: fundamental research, applied research and policy advice. In addition, there is some demand for general enlightment on economic issues by the interested public. This is a fourth market on which economists might be active.

At the time of the classical economists, when economics had not yet established itself as a profession, an economist was a multi-market economist. Now that economics has turned into an industry, each economist specializes in a certain mix of techniques and typically focuses on a specific market. Van Dalen and Klamer distinguish between the academic professional (who aims at obtaining applause from his peers), the researcher (whose objective is to conduct research that is relevant for decision making in policy) and the policy adviser (who seeks to enlighten the policy process and who want his advice accepted). Each market requires its own mix of techniques; the criteria for success differ across markets. As economists, we are well aware of the fact that it pays to specialize. Different markets may require different types of expertise to be successful. For the scientist who wants to extend the stock of knowledge, specialization in a narrow field may be essential. However, the ability to synthesize and generalize may be required to be a successful policy economist.

Of course, the ability to convince others is essential for all types of economists. We may agree with Theeuwes that an economist's objective is to convince others of the value of an idea or insight that he or she has developed. In the academic market one has to convince the editors and referees; in the policy market one has to convince users of the practicality of the idea. Theeuwes's contribution raises the question of whether different marketing techniques are appropriate in different markets. Theeuwes seems to focus on the market for policy advice. He suggests that the policy economist may present the evidence selectively, that is only the evidence that supports the case. He even suggests that an economist may at one time defend one position and at another time the opposite position. Yet, at the same time, Theeuwes insists that the economist be honest. But is the economist who presents selective evidence honest? Is presenting selective evidence allowed in the academic market? Malinvaud disagrees with Theeuwes: 'Economists ... should refrain from taking sides when conclusions are not clearly determined'. Hence, is it really appropriate to compare an economist to a lawyer or should the economist act as a neutral expert?

Not only should different types of economists exhibit different abilities, the applied economist should also master a different set of tools than the pure scientist. Practical economic problems cannot be solved by economic theory alone. It is inevitable that non-economic considerations enter as well. Pure scientific activity differs from problem solving; ultimately, the quality of a piece of applied work is judged by the quality of the solution for the problem that was posed.

Fundamental differences concerning quality and value added exist between the various markets. The scientist adds knowledge, he pushes the knowledge frontier outward. Here analytical capabilities are especially important. The engineer applies existing knowledge so that the ability to synthesize existing knowledge is important. It will be rare that the combination is present in one and the same person. In addition, each market needs its own special expertise. For example, political talent is more important in the policy market than in the academic market. Furthermore, in the policy market one has to be quick, whereas endurance is important in the academic market. It will be very rare indeed for a person to be successful, or be able to compete, in both markets and good economists probably are the rarest of birds.

10.5 Different Types of Funding

Of all contributors to this book, Frey and Eichenberger are the most sobering about the future of economics. They predict that increased global competition will strengthen the incentives to do irrelevant, formal research: economics departments will be transformed into small departments of applied mathematics. While most of their analysis is positive, based on the assumption that economists, and their work, are based on too narrow an objective standard (rigour and elegance), they suggest also that a more broadly based evaluation scheme (in which policy advice is explicitly taken into account) may offer some consolation.

We agree with Portes that users should not dictate the scientific research agenda. At the same time, we believe that we should think hard about new incentive structures that would tilt the balance in favour of applied work. Each scientist is confronted daily with many problems that are internal to the science, because other scientists are eager to communicate their results, which always throw up new problems. However, most academic economists are not in close contact with the practitioner so that they encounter his problems much less frequently. Many relevant real world problems are not communicated directly, but rather through noisy channels such as the media. Couple this observation with Solow's (1989, pp. 39-40) admission that most economists lack a talent for direct observation and it is clear that the probability that an academic economist picks up a relevant, tractable 'real world' problem is much lower than that he picks up a problem communicated by a fellow scientist. Economic science needs the help from practitioners to stay on the right track.

In this respect, intensive communication between academics and practitioners is of the utmost importance. Hence rotation between the different types of jobs might be very beneficial. While users should not dictate the academic research agenda, they should inform scientists about their problems and needs. Of course, given that research takes time, the contacts are especially worthwhile if the information is provided by users with 'Vision', by those who can anticipate the future problems to a certain extent. Certainly, as Geelhoed remarks, policy-makers should not wait until academics have finished their job. In the discussion that followed after his talk, Geelhoed mentioned various European policy issues that he believed would figure prominently in the near future: the debate on location, the economics of public infrastructure, and the impact of EMU in a system of economies with widely differing institutional settings. Economic science should not follow but rather prime the policy debate. In response, Portes argued that curiosity driven research has yielded important insight on location problems and that a lot of research has been done on EMU, driven by the perception of economists that this an important problem. In Chapter 9, Geelhoed discusses the case of CEPR's timely research on the transition of Eastern Europe. Here Geelhoed and Portes agree on both the research agenda's topic and on the need for first class economic research. However, they disagree fundamentally about what is good research. The available research is not Geelhoed's cup of tea. What Portes considers 'first class' is irrelevant in the opinion of Geelhoed.

Instead of reducing the costs of doing relevant research, one may attempt to raise its benefits. In this connection a suggestion made in Tullock (1989) deserves to be taken up. Tullock starts from the observation, also mentioned in Portes' contribution, that the problem arises from the fact that economists generally do not produce exploitable innovations. Consequently, Tullock turns to systems with patentlike properties. He suggests organizing tournaments in order to reward research *ex post*. 'That is, instead of trying to guide the research in advance by research grant proposals, we simply pay people in terms of the potential merit of the research after the research is done. It is easier to judge the value of a research project after it is finished than before it is started' (Tullock 1989, p. 242). Of course, fundamental research is rewarded by a similar process (a publication is not guaranteed at the start). By rewarding also applied research in this way, the quality and quantity of applied research could be raised.

Obviously, given its public good character, the government has an essential responsibility in funding fundamental, curiosly-driven 'blue-sky' research. The trend observed by Portes that government agencies are reducing funds for this type of research and that they insist on societal relevance in addition to, or perhaps even as a substitute for, scientific quality, is somewhat worrying, but understandable. While Geelhoed disagrees with Portes on many aspects, he agrees with him on the value of 'blue-sky' research and he points to risk aversion on the part of funding institutions as a possible explanation why various fundamental questions seem to have received only very limited attention from economists. The Dutch funding agency asks research projects to be evaluated according to their feasibility (a referee has to judge whether one can have confidence that the project will be successfully completed, taking into account the reputation and quality of the proposer and his experience in the field). Obviously, there is nothing wrong with insisting on quality. However, the arguments from Frey and Eichenberger imply that insisting on experience inhibits scientific progress: it makes it more difficult to get funding for innovative research that falls between two rays. Colander (1992, p. 194) argues that current abstract thinking is application of technique to precisely defined problems and that such work seldom leads to significant advances in science. The method of funding, however, is biased in favour of this type of insignificant work.

10.6 Different Types of Teaching

Academic economists have not only been criticized for the perceived lack of relevance of their research; they are also responsible for the training of the future generations of economists and their teaching has been criticized as well. Geelhoed complains that 'whereas 90 per cent of our students do not want to become scientists, both graduate and post graduate education still appear to aim at providing the foundation for a scientific career'. In Geelhoed's opinion, Dutch students are trained in techniques rather than in relevant applications or economic history. Moreover, whereas students are motivated by the problems of the Dutch society, they are trained to solve problems of the US economy. In other words, education caters mainly to the academic market and educators seem most interested in training and selecting good future direct colleagues. Consequently, demand for other types of economists is not met very well so that new entrants into the Dutch administration have to be retrained.

In Malinvaud's view the main criticism is that teaching gives too much attention to abstract problems and too little attention to the most pressing problems of modern society. There is a 'mismatch between the supply of knowledge to students and the demand of society with respect to what students ought to know'. In his view two other supply-side problems are that teaching focuses on theory out of context (the emphasis is on the pure theory without discussing the empirical foundations so that students do not have a good idea about the domain of relevance of a theory) and that teaching concentrates too much on fads and fashions in economic research. A larger distance from current research is preferable since it gives more insight and reduces the need for formalism: teaching should concentrate on the ideas that have already proved themselves.

This mismatch originates in the incentives that university teachers face. Evaluation is based mainly on scientific achievement whereas teaching consumes research time. The 'time lost' is minimized by focusing teaching on issues that are as close to research as possible. Similarly, since academics profit directly from well trained colleagues, it is natural that they focus their effort on it, unless incentives are in place that induce them to do otherwise. Given that 90 per cent of the students finds a job outside of academia, it is surprising that such incentives apparently are either absent or weak. Either the retraining by employers that Geelhoed refers to is efficient or competition in the market for education is lacking.

One reason for insufficient competition might be a lack of information. Hence job mobility might help because economists who have worked on both sides might provide a clearer perspective on the necessary ingredients of education. Harberger (1993, p. 22) notes that economic education 'should import the type of simple and robust theoretical framework that economists will be able to use for the rest of their lives, and also how to use it'. Since applied economists have to be able to respond quickly, they have to be able to think on their feet. Therefore, they have to know simple tools and how to use them well. Indeed, economic education should train students to 'think like an economist'.

Probably education currently focuses too much on introducing new tools without showing how these tools can be applied to real world issues. Economists seem to believe that knowledge of the tools automatically yields knowledge about when and how a tool can be used. Schumpeter already noted that this is a misunderstanding:

> Everybody knows that in order to play chess it is not enough to know the figures and how they move. It should be equally clear that the mere knowledge of definitions and theorems is not enough to play the scientific game ... what one ought to learn is to work with such theories, how to analyze concrete situations and how to solve problems with them. (Schumpeter 1982, p. 1059 and p. 1055)

In Schumpeter's view, the training in the handling of economic tools (and in particular theories) should be the essential task of economic education. He believes much of teaching is deficient in this respect. Even among professional economists, 'thoroughly competent ones are comparatively rare ... current discussion of economic questions almost always displays the sad fact that some and occasionally all who take a hand in it do not know what they are talking about' (p. 1058). These discussions 'are all like duels between combatants who have not learned the art of fencing' (p. 1052).

The discussion above does not necessarily conflict with the view of Frey and Eichenberger that policy advice essentially requires core economics. However, it makes it doubtful whether the core can be taught in one semester. Perhaps the essence of the core (that is, rational behaviour and the resulting equilibrium) can be taught in just one semester, but by then one knows only the rules of the game, not how the game is played (or could be played) and what insights could be gained by playing it. One needs considerably more time to learn how to use these basic tools and how to use them well. After all, there is no demand for students that have attended courses for only one semester. Even when the useful economic principles are simple, it might take considerable training and experience in applying, before their strengths and limitations are sufficiently understood.

We agree with Schumpeter (1982, p. 1054) that 'it is no advantage for a science to be too easy, for this will deter good and attract mediocre minds and create a strong party of opposition to achievement and refinement'. Indeed economics suffers from the fact that not everybody realizes that

> economics is not a doctrine which one might accept or reject but rather an arsenal of theoretical tools which you have to train yourself to use before you can have any opinion about its usefulness or otherwise and that many of the shortcomings of the science are caused by the incompetence of very many economists, who never learned their own business and turn to politics and philosophy because they are not up to the task of the scientist (Schumpeter, 1982, p. 1053).

Economic education, in our view, should focus on the training of the use of the tools. At the same time it should convince students that these tools are powerful enough to enrich the understanding of the real world.

10.7 Different Types of Conclusions

Different conclusions can be drawn from the material presented here. One obvious conclusion is that the (ir)relevance of economics is a difficult subject; that the problem, if there is one, may not have an obvious solution. The market for economic research may not work perfectly, but it is not crystal clear how it could be made to work better.

Portes and Frey and Eichenberger present the two extreme views in this book. Frey and Eichenberger argued that something is fundamentally wrong with our discipline and that something needs to be done about it. We argued that their analysis may be based on shaky foundations and that their policy recommendations need not lead to improvement. Portes, in contrast, believes that the market works perfectly and argues accordingly. We are not convinced by his arguments that the self-regulating mechanisms of the profession can be relied upon. Actually, it is somewhat strange that, at a time when economists (as 'guardians of sound principles') advocate deregulation of many sectors of the economy and thereby point out the dangers inherent in self-regulation, one distinguished economist essentially backs up his arguments by relying on the virtues of the self-regulatory mechanism for his own profession. The laws of economics apply to economics as well. Hence, as economists we should accept that the satisfaction of demand is the acid test that we should meet. Accordingly, the fact that users complain should concern us.

Thusfar we have restricted ourselves to setting straight, to pointing out which problems are real and which ones result from misperceptions. We have argued that, when one takes a detailed look, many problems are only perceived. Hence, these problems could be resolved by improved communication between the various stake-holders in economics. Indeed, a plea for improved communication has been a thread running throughout this chapter.

A second thread has been that there is no point in lumping everything and everyone together: we need diversity! Policy engineering as well as the 'guarding of sound principles' can play a useful role in policy-making. Both applied research and purely speculative 'blue-sky' research serve an important purpose. The science of economics should be distinguished from its applications; if the engineering part, perhaps, is not very successful, the baby (the science) should not be thrown out with the bath water; science can stand by itself. Diffusion of knowledge is important, just as innovation is. Moreover, we should recognize the bounded and different capacities of individuals so that we can exploit differences in talent as much as possible. Different markets require different skills. Very few people are good at more than one thing. Hence specialization pays.

Our advice amounts to recognizing the advantages of specialization and to exploit these advantages as much as possible by allowing for free trade and competition in ideas. As economists, we believe that competition may improve efficiency. Indeed, we have not been fully convinced by Frey and Eichenberger that intensified competition has adverse effects, although we take their analysis as a serious warning that we should carefully analyse the structure of the market for economic ideas. Clearly, for trade to occur, communication is necessary and we suggest removing barriers to the exchange of ideas. By improving communication channels, the information base and the transparency of the markets may increase and this, in turn, may lead to intensified competition with positive effects.

References

Akerlof, G., 1984, 'The market for "lemons": Quality, uncertainty and the market mechanism', *Quarterly Journal of Economics* **84** (3), pp. 488-500.

Alchian, A.A., 1977, *Economic Forces at Work,* Indianapolis: Liberty.

Allen, W.R., 1977, 'Economics, Economists, and Economic Policy: Modern American Experiences', *History of Political Economy* **9**, pp. 48-88.

Alston, R.M., J.R. Kearl and M.B. Vaughn, 1992, 'Is There a Global Consensus Among Economists in the 1990s?', *American Economic Review*, Papers and Proceedings, **82** (2), pp. 203-9.

Aoki, M., 1995, 'Towards comparative institutional analysis', in: A. Heertje (ed.), *The Makers of Modern Economics*, vol. 2, Aldershot: Edward Elgar, pp. 47-67.

Arrow, K.J., 1951, *Social Choice and Individual Values*, New York: John Wiley & Sons.

Arrow, K.J., 1995, 'Foreword', in: G.B. Shepard (ed.), *Rejected. Leading Economists Ponder the Publication Process*, Sun Lakes: Horton.

Arrow, K.J., R.S. Solow, E. Leamer, P. Portney, R. Radner and H. Schuman, 1993, 'Report of the NOAA-Panel on Contingent Valuation', *Federal Register*, **58** (10), pp. 4601-14.

Arthur, W.B., 1989, 'Competing Technologies, Increasing Returns, and Lock-In by Historical Events', *Economic Journal*, **99**, pp. 116-31.

Aumann, R., 1985, 'What is Game Theory Trying to Accomplish?', in: K.J. Arrow and S. Honkapohja (eds), *Frontiers of Economics*, Oxford and New York: Basil Blackwell, pp. 28-76.

Baker, J.B., 1993, 'Two Scherman Act Section I Dilemmas: Parallel Pricing, the Oligopoly Problem, and Contemporary Economic Theory', *The Antitrust Bulletin*, **38** (1), pp. 143-219.

Barro, R.J., 1993, 'Council of Economic Irrelevance', *Wall Street Journal,* Tuesday, January 12.

Barros, P. and L. Cabral, 1994, 'Merger Policy in Open Economics', *European Economic Review,* **38** (5), pp. 1041-46.

Baumol, W.J., 1995, 'What is different about European Economics?' *Kyklos,* **48** (2), pp. 187-92.

Bean, C., 1994, 'European Unemployment: A Survey', *Journal of Economic Literature,* **32** (2), pp. 573-619.

Beaudry, P. and J. DiNardo, 1991, 'The Effect of Implicit Contracts on the Movement of Wages over the Business Cycle', *Journal of Political Economy,* **99** (4), pp. 665-88.

Becker, G.S., 1976, *The Economic Approach to Human Behavior,* Chicago: Chicago University Press.

Begg, D.A. et al., 1990, 'The East, the Deutschmark and EMU', in: *Monitoring European Integration: The impact of Eastern Europe,* London: CEPR, pp. 31-67.

Bergeijk, P.A.G. van, A.L. Bovenberg, E.E.C. van Damme and J. van Sinderen (eds), 1997, *Economic Science: An Art or an Asset? The Case of the Netherlands* Rotterdam: OCFEB.

Bergeijk, P.A.G. van and R. Lensink, 1993, 'Trade, Capital and the Transition in Central Europe,' *Applied Economics,* **25** (7), pp. 891-903.

Bergh, T., 1981, 'Norway: The Powerful Servants', *History of Political Economy,* **13** (3), pp. 471-512.

Bergman, B.R., 1989, 'Why do Economists Know so Little About the Economy?', in: S. Bowles, R. Edwards and W.G. Shepard (eds), *Unconventional Wisdom: Essays in Honor of John Kenneth Galbraith.* Boston: Houghton Mifflin, pp. 29-38.

Besanko, D. and D. Spulber, 1989, 'Antitrust Enforcement Under Asymmetric Information', *Economic Journal,* **99**, pp. 408-25.

Black, D., 1948, 'On the Rationale of Group Decision Making', *Journal of Political Economy,* **56**, pp. 23-34.

Blaug, M., 1975, *The Cambrige Revolution. Success or Failure?,* London: Institute of Economic Affairs.

Block, W. and M. Walker, 1988, 'Entropy in the Canadian Economics Profession', *Canadian Public Policy* **14**, pp. 137-50.

Bobe, B. and A. Etchegoyen, 1981, *Economistes en désordre: Consensus et dissensions,* Paris: Economica.

Bohnet, I. and B.S. Frey, 1995, 'Ist Reden Silber und Schweigen Gold? Eine ökonomische Analyse', *Zeitschrift für Wirtschafts- und Sozialwissenschaften* **115**, pp. 169-209.

Bork, R., 1967, 'The Goals of Antitrust Policy', *American Economic Review*, **57** (2), pp. 242-53.

Boyer, E.L., P.G. Altbach and M.Y. Whitelaw, 1994, *The Academic Profession: An International Perspective*, Ewing (New Jersey): Carnegie Foundation for the Advancement of Teaching.

Brennan, D.G. (ed.), 1961, *Arms Control, Disarmament and National Security*, New York: George Braziller.

Bresnahan, T.F., 1989, 'Empirical studies of industries with market power', in R. Schmalensee and R. Wilby (eds), *Handbook of Industrial Organisation*, vol. 2, Amsterdam: North Holland, pp. 1011-58.

Brown, C., C. Gilroy and A. Kohen, 1982, 'The Effect of the Minimum Wage on Employment and Unemployment', *Journal of Economic Literature*, **20** (2), pp. 487-528.

Buchanan, J.M., 1995, 'Economic Science and Cultural Diversity', *Kyklos*, **48** (2), pp. 193-200.

Buigues, P., A. Jacquemin and A. Sapir, 1995, *European Policies on Competition, Trade and Industry: Conflict and Complementarities*, Cheltenham: Edward Elgar.

Bull, H., 1961, *The Control of the Arms Race*, London: Institute for Strategic Studies.

Card, D.E. and A.B. Krueger, 1994, 'Minimum Wages and Employment: A Case Study of the Fast-Food Industry in New Jersey and Pennsylvania', *American Economic Review*, **84** (4), pp. 772-93.

Card, D.E. and A.B. Krueger, 1995, *Myth and Measurement. The New Economics of the Minimum Wage*, Princeton: Princeton University Press.

Chamberlin, E., 1933, *The Theory of Monopolistic Competition*, Cambridge (Mass.): Harvard University Press.

Cigno, A., 1991, *Economics of the Family*, Oxford: Oxford University Press.

Coe, O.T. and H. Helpman, 1993, *International R&D Spillovers, CEPR Discussion Paper 840*, London: CEPR.

Colander, D., 1989, 'Research on the Economics Profession', *Journal of Economic Perspectives*, **4** (Fall), pp. 137-48.

Colander, D., 1991, *Why aren't Economists as Important as Garbagemen?*, London: Sharpe.

Colander, D., 1992, 'Retrospects: The lost art of economics', *Journal of Economic Perspectives*, **6** (3), pp. 191-8.

Colander, D. and A. Klamer, 1987, 'The Making of an Economist', *Journal of Economic Perspectives*, **1** (Fall), pp. 95-111.

Coley, S. and S. Reiton, 1988, 'The Hunt for Value', *McKinsey Quarterly*, Spring.

Commission of the European Communities, 1972, *Report on competition policy*, Brussels.

D'Aspremont, C. and A. Jacquemin, 1988, 'Cooperative and Non-Cooperative R&D Industry with Spillovers', *American Economic Review*, **78** (5), pp. 1133-7.

D'Aspremont, C. and A. Jacquemin, 1990, 'Cooperative and Non-Cooperative R&D Industry with Spillovers: erratum,' *American Economic Review*, **80** (3), pp. 641-2.

Dalen, H.P. van, 1997, 'Measuring Giants and Dwarfs; Assessing the Quality of Economists', *Scientometrics*, **38**, pp. 231-52

Dalen, H.P. van, and A. Klamer, 1996a, *Telgen van Tinbergen*, Amsterdam: Uitgeverij Balans.

Dalen, H.P. van and A. Klamer, 1996b, 'De waarden van Nederlandse economen', *ESB*, **81**, pp. 444-8.

Domar, E.D., 1946, 'Capital Expansion, Rate of Growth and Employment', *Econometrica*, **14**, pp. 137-47.

Drèze, J., 1995, 'Forty Years of Public Economics', *Journal of Economic Perspectives*, **9** (2), pp. 111-130.

Duisenberg, W.F., 1997, 'Preface' in: P.A.G. van Bergeijk, A.L. Bovenberg, E.E.C. van Damme and J. van Sinderen (eds), 1997, *Economic Science: An Art or an Asset? The Case of the Netherlands*, Rotterdam: OCFEB.

Edwards, C.P., 1967, *Control of Cartels and Monopolies: An International Comparison*, New York: Oceana Publications.

Eggertsson, T., 1995, 'On the Economics of Economics', *Kyklos*, **48** (2), pp. 201-10.

Eichenberger, R. and F. Oberholzer, 1995, 'Thou shalt not steal: Morale and the Politics of Redistribution', Paper presented at the European Public Choice Society, Saarbrücken, April 19-22.

Ellisson, G., 1994, 'Theories of Cartel Stability and the Joint

Executive Committee', *Rand Journal of Economics*, **25** (1), pp. 37-57.

European Commission, 1996, *Green paper on innovation*, Brussel.

Farrell, J. and C. Shapiro, 1990, 'Horizontal Mergers', *American Economic Review*, **80** (1), pp. 107-26.

Farrell, J. and C. Shapiro, 1991, 'Horizontal Mergers: Reply', *American Economic Review*, **81** (1), pp. 1007-11.

Faulhaber, G.R. and W.J. Baumol, 1988, 'Economists as Innovators', *Journal of Economic Literature*, **26** (2), pp. 577-600.

Feyerabend, P., 1995, *Zeitverschwendung*, Frankfurt: Suhrkamp.

Figlio, D., 1994, 'Trends in the publication of empirical economics', *Journal of Economic Perspectives*, **8** (3), pp. 179-187.

Fisher, F.M., 1989, 'Games Economists Play: A Noncooperative View', *Rand Journal of Economics* **20** (1), pp. 113-24.

Frech III, H.E., 1995, 'European vs. American Economics, Artificial Intelligence and Scientific Content', *Kyklos* **48** (2), pp. 219-30.

Frey, B.S., 1992, *Economics as a Science of Human Behaviour*, Boston and Dordrecht: Kluwer.

Frey, B.S., 1997a, *Not Just for the Money: An Economic Theory of Personal Motivation*, Cheltenham: Edward Elgar.

Frey, B.S., 1997b, 'On the Relationship between Intrinsic and Extrinsic Work Motivation', *International Journal of Industrial Economics*, **15** (July): forthcoming.

Frey, B.S. and I. Bohnet, 1995, 'Institutions Affect Fairness: Experimental Investigations', *Journal of Institutional and Theoretical Economics*, **151** (2), pp. 286-303.

Frey, B.S. and I. Bohnet, 1996, 'Experiments: Theory and Reality. Ökonomie und Gesellschaft', *Jahrbuch 13: Experiments in Economics - Experimente in der Ökonomie*, Frankfurt: Campus.

Frey, B.S. and R. Eichenberger, 1992, 'Economics and economists: A European view', *American Economic Review* **82**, pp. 216-20.

Frey, B.S. and R. Eichenberger, 1993, 'American and European Economics and Economists', *Journal of Economic Perspectives* **9** (4), pp. 185-94.

Frey, B.S., and W.W. Pommerehne, 1988, 'The American Domination Among Eminent Economists', *Scientometrics* 14, 97-110.

Frey, B.S. and W.W. Pommerehne, 1988, 'Für wie fair gilt der

Markt? Eine empirische Untersuchung von Einschätzungen in der Bevölkerung', *Hamburger Jahrbuch für Wirtschafts- und Gesellschaftspolitik*, **33**, pp. 223-37.

Frey, B.S., W.W. Pommerehne, F. Schneider, and G. Gilbert, 1984, 'Consensus and Dissension Among Economists: An Empirical Enquiry', *American Economic Review*, **74**, pp. 986-94.

Frey, B.S., W.W. Pommerehne, F. Schneider and H. Weck, 1982, 'Welche Ansichten vertreten Schweizer Ökonomen?', *Schweizerische Zeitschrift für Volkswirtschaft und Statistik* **118**, pp. 1-40.

Friedman, M. 1953, 'The Methodology of Positive Economics', in: M. Friedman, *Essays in Positive Economics*, Chicago: University of Chicago Press.

Friedman, M., 1994, 'Correspondence', *Journal of Economic Perspectives*, **8** (Winter), pp. 199-200.

Fuchs, V.R., 1996, 'Economics, Values, and Health Care Reform', *American Economic Review*, **86** (1), pp. 1-24.

Galbraith, J.K., 1972, *A Contemporary Guide to Economics, Peace and Laughter*, New York: Signet.

Gans, J.S. and G.B. Shepard, 1994, 'How are the Mighty Fallen: Rejected Classic Articles by Leading Economists', *Journal of Economic Perspectives* **8** (1), pp. 165-79.

Gastil, R., 1989, *Freedom in the World: Political Rights and Civil Liberties 1988-89*, Lanham: Freedom House.

Gelauff, G.M.M. and J.J. Graafland, 1994, *Modelling Welfare State Reform*, North Holland: Amsterdam.

Gent, C. van, 1997, 'New Dutch competition policy: A revolution without revolutionaries', in: P.A.G. van Bergeijk et al. (eds), 1997, *Economic Science: An Art or an Asset? The Case of the Netherlands* Rotterdam: OCFEB [in print].

Gilbert, F. and D. Newbery, 1982, 'Pre-emptive Patenting and the Persistence of Monopoly', *American Economic Review*, **72** (3), 514-26.

Graafland, J.J., 1990, Persistent Unemployment, Wages and Hysteresis, Ph.D. Thesis, Erasmus University Rotterdam.

Hahn, F.H. and R.C.O. Mathews, 1964, 'The Theory for Economic Growth: A Survey', *The Economic Journal*, **74**, pp. 779-903.

Hall, A.D., 1990, 'Worldwide rankings of research activity in econometrics: An update 1980-1988', *Econometric Theory*, **6**, pp.

1-16.

Hamermesh, D.S., 1994, 'Facts and Myths about Refereeing', *Journal of Economic Perspectives,* **8** (1), pp. 153-64.

Hamilton, L.H., 1992, 'Economists as Public Policy Advisers', *Journal of Economic Perspective,* **6** (Summer), pp. 61-4.

Hansen, W.L., 1991, 'The Education and Training of Economics Doctorates' *Journal of Economic Literature,* **29** (3), pp. 1054-87.

Harberger, A.C., 1993, 'The Search for Relevance in Economics', *American Economic Review,* **83** (2), pp. 1-16.

Harcourt, G.C., 1972, *Some Cambridge Controversies in the Theory of Capital,* Cambridge: Cambridge University Press.

Harrod, R.F., 1939, 'An Essay in Dynamic Theory', *Economic Journal,* **49**, pp. 14-33.

Hartog, J. and J.J.M. Theeuwes, 1993, 'Post-war Unemployment in the Netherlands', *European Journal of Political Economy* **9** (1), pp. 73-112.

Hasenberg-Butter, I., 1969, *Academic Economics in Holland, 1800-1870,* The Hague: Martinus Nijhoff.

Hassink, W.H.J. (1996), *Worker Flows and the Employment Adjustment of Firms,* Amsterdam: Thesis Publishers.

Heclo, H. and A. Wildavsky, 1974, *The Private Government of Public Money,* Macmillan: London.

Henderson, D., 1986, *Innocence and Design: The Influence of Economic Ideas on Policy,* Oxford and New York: Blackwell.

Herrnstein, R.J. and C. Murray, 1994, *The Bell Curve: Intelligence and class structure in American life,* Free Press: New York.

Holub, H.W., 1989, 'Theory versus Empiricism in Academic Economics: Comment', *Journal of Economic Perspectives,* **3** (4), pp. 207-9.

Holub, H.W., 1990, 'Die PME-Ökonomik. Ein kleiner Beitrag zur jüngsten historischen Schule', *Wirtschaftswissenschaftliches Studium,* **19**, p. 296.

Holub, H.W., 1992, 'Die Rolle der PME-Ökonomik im Wirtschaftsbetrieb', *Jahrbücher für Nationalökonomie und Statistik,* **210**, pp. 332-5.

Holub, H.W., G. Tappeiner and V. Eberharter, 1991, 'The Iron Law of Important Articles', *Southern Economic Journal,* **58** (2), pp. 317-28.

Hulshof, M.J.F., A.H.M. Verrijt and A. Kruijthoff, 1996, *Promoveren en de arbeidsmarkt*, The Hague: OCenW.

Hutton, W. and P. Couglan, 1995, 'The state we're in', *Economics and Business Education*, **3** (2), p. 87.

Jacquemin, A., 1987, *The New Industrial Organisation: Market forces and strategic behavior*, Cambridge: MIT Press.

Jacquemin, A. and M.E. Slade, 1989, 'Cartels, collusion and horizontal merger', in: R. Schmalensee and R. Wilby (eds), *Handbook of Industrial Organisation*, Amsterdam: North Holland, pp. 415-73.

Jenny, F., 1992, 'Competition and Competition Policy', in: W.J. Adams (ed.), *Singular Europe: Economy and Polity of the European Community after 1992*, University of Michigan Press: Michigan, pp. 69-95.

Kagel, J. and A.E. Roth, 1995, *Handbook of Experimental Economics*, Princeton: Princeton University Press.

Kapteijn, A. and A. de Zeeuw, 1991, 'Changing incentives for economic research in the Netherlands', *European Economic Review,* **35**, pp. 603-11.

Kearl, J.R., C.L. Pope, G.L. Whiting and L.T. Wimmer, 1979, 'A Confusion of Economists?', *American Economic Review*, **69**, pp. 28-37.

Keynes, J.N., 1891, *The scope and method of political economy* 4th edition, Macmillan: London.

Kirman, A. and M. Dahl, 1994, 'Economic Research in Europe', *European Economic Review*, **38** (3-4), pp. 505-22.

Klamer, A., 1990, *Verzuilde dromen*, Balans: Amsterdam.

Klamer, A., 1995, 'A Rhetorical Perspective on the Differences Between European and American Economists', *Kyklos*, **48** (2), pp. 231-40.

Klamer, A. and D. Colander, 1990, *The Making of An Economist*, Boulder, Westview Press.

Klamer, A. and J. Meehan, 1994, 'The Crowding Out of Academic Economists', mimeo, George Washington University.

Kolm, S.-C., 1988, 'Economics in Europe and in the U.S.', *European Economic Review*, **32**, pp. 207-12.

Krueger, A.O. et al., 1991, 'Report of the Commission on Graduate Education in Economics', *Journal of Economic Literature* **29** (3), pp. 1035-53.

Krugman, P., 1994, *Peddling Prosperity, Economic Sense and Non-Sense in the Age of Diminished Expectations*, Norton: New York.

Krugman, P., 1995, 'Incidents from my career', in: A. Heertje (ed.), *The Makers of Modern Economics*, vol. 2, Aldershot: Edward Elgar, pp. 29-46.

Krugman, P., 1996, *Pop Internationalism*, Cambridge (Mass.): MIT Press.

Kühn, K.U. and X. Vives, 1994, 'Information exchanges among firms and their impact on competition', Working Paper, European Commission (DG.IV): Brussel

Lazonick, W., 1991, *Business Organization and the Myth of the Market Economy*, Cambridge: Cambridge University Press.

Leamer, E., 1983, 'Let's Take the Con out of Econometrics', *American Economic Review*, 73, pp. 31-43.

Leijonhufvud, A., 1973, 'Life Among the Econ', *Western Economic Journal*, 11 (September), pp. 327-37.

Levine, R. and D. Renelt, 1992, 'A Sensitivity Analysis of Cross-Country Growth Regression' *American Economic Review* 82 (4), pp. 942-63.

Lewin, S., 1996, 'Economics and Psychology', *Journal of Economic Literature*, 34 (3), pp. 1293-1323.

Lindbeck, A., 1985, 'The prize in economic science in memory of Alfred Nobel', *Journal of Economic Literature*, 23 (1), pp. 37-56.

Lindbeck, A., 1995, 'Hazardous welfare-state dynamics', *American Economic Review*.

Lubbers Committee (Verkenningscommissie Economische Weten-schappen), 1996, *Kijk op economische kennis*, Ministry of Education and Science, The Hague.

Lucas, R.E., 1976, 'Econometric Policy Evaluations: A Critique', *Journal of Monetary Economics* Suppl. (April) (K. Brunner and E. Meltze (eds)), pp. 19-46.

Magnus, J.R. and M.S. Morgan, 1987, 'The ET Interview: Professor J. Tinbergen', *Econometric Theory*, 3, pp. 117-142.

Mäki, U., 1995, 'Diagnosing McCloskey', *Journal of Economic Literature*, 33 (3), pp. 1300-18.

Malinvaud, E., 1995, 'Why economists do not make discoveries', International Economic Association Congress, Tunis, December.

Marshall, A., 1890, *The Principles of Economics* (8th edition), Macmillan: London and Basingstoke.

Martin, S., 1993, *Advanced Industrial Economics,* Oxford and Cambridge (Mass.): Blackwell.

Mayer, T., 1993, *Truth versus Percision in Economics*, Aldershot: Edward Elgar.

McCloskey, D.N., 1983, 'The Rhetoric of Economics,' *Journal of Economic Literature*, **21** (2), pp. 481-517.

McCloskey, D.N., 1987, 'Rhetoric', in: J. Eatwell, M. Milgate and P. Newman (eds), *The New Palgrave. A Dictionary of Economics*, London: Macmillan, pp. 173-4.

McCloskey, D.N., 1996, *The Vices of Economists; The Virtues of the Bourgeoisie*, Amsterdam University Press: Amsterdam.

McKenzie, R.B. and G. Tullock, 1975, *The New World of Economics*, 2nd ed. Homewood, Ill.: Irwin.

Mestmacker, E.J., 1980, 'Competition Policy and Antitrust: Some comparative observations', *Weitschrift für die gesamte Staatswissenschaft - JITE*, **136** (3), pp. 387-407.

Milgrom, P. and J. Roberts, 1988, 'Economic Theories of the Firm, past, present and future', *Canadian Journal of Economics*, **21** (3), pp. 444-58.

Ministry of Social Affairs and Employment, 1996, *De Nederlandse verzorgingsstaat in internationaal en economisch perspectief*, SDU Uitgevers: The Hague.

Morgan, M.S., 1988, 'Finding a Satisfactory Empirical Model', in: N. de Marchi (ed.), *The Popperian Legacy in Economics*, Cambridge University Press, Cambridge.

Morgan, M.S., 1990, *History of Econometric Ideas*, Cambridge: Cambridge University Press.

Morgan, T., 1988, 'Theory versus Empiricism in Academic Economics: Update and Comparisons', *Journal of Economic Perspectives*, **2** (4), pp. 159-64.

Mueller, D.C., 1989, 'Mergers, Causes, Effects and Policies', *International Journal of Industrial Organisation*, **7** (1), pp. 1-10.

Norman, G. and M. La Manna, 1992, (eds), *The New Industrial Economics,* Aldershot: Edward Elgar

Nyfer, 1996, *Jaarverslag Nederland*, The Hague: SDU.

OECD, 1995, *The Jobs Study*, Paris: OECD.

Oldersma, H.A. and P.A.G. van Bergeijk, 1992, 'The Potential for an Export-oriented Growth Strategy in Central Europe', *Journal of World Trade*, **26** (4), pp. 47-63.

Ordover, J.A. and W.J. Baumol, 1988, 'Antitrust Policy and High-Technology Industries', *Oxford Review of Economic Policy*, **4** (4), pp. 13-34

Ormerod, P., 1994, *The Death of Economics*, London: Faber and Faber.

Osterloh, M., S. Grand and R. Tiemann, 1994, 'Modelling or Mapping? Von Rede- und Schweigeinstrumenten in der betriebswissenschaftslichen Forschung', *Die Unternehmung*, **48**, pp. 277-94.

Ours, J.C. van, 1991, 'The Efficiency of the Dutch Labour Market in Matching Unemployment and Vacancies', *De Economist*, **139** (3), pp. 359-78.

Phelps, E., 1995, 'A Life in Economics', in: A. Heertje (ed.), *The Makers of Modern Economics*, vol. 2, Aldershot: Edward Elgar, pp. 90-113.

Ploeg, F. van der, 1992, *Is de econoom een vijand van het volk?*, Amsterdam University Press: Amsterdam.

Pommerehne, W.W., F. Schneider and B.S. Frey, 1983, 'Quot homines, tot sententiae? A survey among Austrian economists', *Empirica*, pp. 93-127.

Pommerehne, W.W., F. Schneider, G. Gilbert and B.S. Frey, 1984, 'Concordia Discors: Or: What do Economists Think?' *Theory and Decision*, **16**, pp. 251-308.

Porter, R., 1983, 'A Study of Cartel Stability: The joint Executive Committee 1880-1886', *Bell Journal of Economics* **14** (2), pp. 301-14.

Portes, R., 1987, 'Economics in Europe', *European Economic Review* **31**, pp. 1329-40.

Reinganum, S.F., 1983, 'Uncertain Innovation and the Persistence of Monopoly: Reply', *American Economic Review* **83** (4), pp. 741-48.

Ricketts, M. and E. Shoesmith, 1990, *British Economic Opinion*, Institute of Economic Affairs: London.

Ricketts, M. and E. Shoesmith, 1992, 'British Economic Opinion: Positive Science or Normative Judgement?' *American Economic*

Review, Papers and Proceedings **80**, pp. 210-5.

Robinson, J. 1939, *The Economics of Imperfect Competition*, Macmillan: London.

Rumelt, R.P., D. Schendel and D.J. Teece, 1991, 'Strategic Management and Economics', *Strategic Management Journal*, **12**, pp. 5-29.

Samuelson, P., 1962, 'Economists and the History of Ideas', *American Economic Review*, **52** (1), pp. 1-18.

Schelling, T.C. and M.H. Halperin, 1961, *Strategy and Arms Control*, New York: The Twentieth Century Fund.

Schmalensee, R., 1987, 'Horizontal Merger Policy: Problems and Changes', *Journal of Economic Perspectives*, **1** (2), pp. 41-51.

Schneider, F., W.W. Pommerehne and B.S. Frey, 1983, 'Relata Referimus: Eine Befragung deutscher Ökonomen', *Journal for Institutional and Theoretical Economics*, **139** (March), pp. 19-66.

Schumpeter, J., 1950, *Capitalism, Socialism and Democracy*, London: Allen and Unwin

Schumpeter, J.A., 1954, *History of Economic Analysis, Oxford University Press*, London: Allen & Unwin.

Schumpeter, J.A., [1931] 1982, 'The "Crises" in Economics - Fifty years ago', *Journal of Economic Literature*, **20**, pp. 1049-59.

Scully, G.W., 1992, *Constitutional Environments and Economic Growth*, Princeton: Princeton University Press.

Sen, A.K., 1970, *Collective Choice and Social Welfare*, Edinburgh and London: Oliver & Boyd.

Shapiro, C., 1989, 'Theories of Oligopoly Behaviour', in R. Schmalensee and R.D. Willig (eds), *Handbook of Industrial Organisation*, vol. 1, Amsterdam: North Holland, pp. 329-414.

Shepard, G.B. (ed.), 1995, *Rejected. Leading Economists Ponder the Publication Process*. Sun Lakes: Horton.

Shubik M., 1985, 'What is game theory trying to accomplish' in: K.J. Arrow and S. Honkapohja (eds), *Frontiers of Economics*, Oxford and New York: Basil Blackwell, pp. 88-95.

Sinderen, J. van, 1992, *Over pre-economen, beleidseconomen en wetenschappers*, Rotterdam: Erasmus Universiteit.

Slade, M., 1987, 'Interfirm Rivalry in a Repeated Game: An Empirical Test of Tacit Collusion', *Journal of Industrial Economics*, **35**, pp. 499-516.

Smart, S. and J. Waldfogel, 1996, 'A Citation-Based Test for Discrimination at Economics and Finance Journals', *NBER Working Paper 5460*, Cambridge (Mass.): NBER.

Smets, H. and P. van Cayseele, 1995, 'Competing Merger Policies in a Common Agency Framework', *International Review of Law and Economics*, **15** (4), pp. 499-516.

Smith, A., 1776, *An Inquiry into the Nature and Causes of the Wealth of Nations*, Canna's edition, Oxford: Clarendon Press.

Solow, R.M., 1956, 'A Contribution to the Theory of Economic Growth', *Quarterly Journal of Economics*, **70**, pp. 65-94.

Solow, R.M., 1957, 'Technical change and the aggregate production function', *Review of Economics and Statistics*, **39**, pp. 312-20.

Solow, R.M., 1967, 'The New Industrial State or Sons of Affluence', *Public Interest*, **9** (Fall), pp. 100-8.

Solow, R.M., 1989, 'Faith, hope and clarity', in: D. Colander and A.W. Coats (eds), *The spread of economic ideas*, Cambridge: Cambridge University press, pp. 37-41.

Stigler, G.J., 1955, 'The Nature and Role of Orginality in Scientific Progress', reprinted in G.J. Stigler, 1965, *Essays in the History of Economic Ideas*, University of Chicago Press, Chicago.

Stigler, G.J., 1963, *The Intellectual and the Market Place and Other Essays*, London and Basingstoke: Macmillan.

Summers, L.H., 1991, 'The Scientific Illusion in Empirical Macroeconomics', *Scandinavian Journal of Economics* **93**, pp. 129-48.

Summers, R. and A. Heston, 1991, 'The Penn World Table (Mark 5)', *Quarterly Journal of Economics*, **106** (2), pp. 327-68.

Tabellini, G., 1995, 'The Organization of Economic Research: Why Europe is Still Behind', *Kyklos* **48**, pp. 297-302.

Taylor, J., and H. Izadi, 1996, 'The 1992 Research Assessment Exercise: Outcome, Outputs and Inputs in Economics and Econometrics', *Bulletin of Economic Research* **48**, pp. 1-26.

Teulings, C.N., 1990, 'Conjunctuur en kwalificatie', Ph.D. Thesis University of Amsterdam.

Teulings, C.N. and J. Hartog 1997, *Corporatism or Competition? Labour Market Contracts and Institutions in International Comparison*, Cambridge: Cambridge University Press.

Theeuwes, J.J.M., 1995, 'Beweeglijk werk', *ESB* **80**, pp. 1152-54.

Throsby, D.C., 1994, 'The Production and Consumption of the

Arts', *Journal of Economic Literature* **33**, pp. 1-29.

Tinbergen, J., 1952, *On the Theory of Economic Policy*, Amsterdam: North-Holland.

Tinbergen, J., 1979, 'Recollections of Professional Experiences', *Banca Nazionale del Lavoro Quarterly Review*, **131**, pp. 331-60.

Tirole, J., 1989, *The Theory of Industrial Organisation,* Cambridge (Mass.): MIT Press

Torre, A., 1990, 'Quand les Economistes mesurent l'Intangible', *Revue d'Economie Industrielle*, **53**.

Towse, R. and M. Blaug, 1990, 'The Current State of the British Economic Profession', *Economic Journal* **100**, pp. 227-36.

Tullock, G., 1989, 'Changing incentives to make economics more relevant', in: D. Colander et al. (eds), *The spread of economic ideas*, Cambridge: Cambridge University press, pp. 235-47.

Vries, B. de, 1995, 'Een halve eeuw werk, werk en de werking van de arbeidsmarkt', Research Memorandum, Rotterdam: OCFEB.

VSNU, 1995, *Quality Assessment of Research - Economics*, Vereniging Samenwerkende Nederlandse Universiteiten:, Utrecht.

Winden, F. van, 1995, 'On European Economics' *Kyklos* **48** (2), pp. 303-11.

Weinstein, N.D., 1980, 'Unrealistic optimism about future life events', *Journal of Personality and Social Psychology* **39**, pp. 806-20.

Werden, G.J., 1991, 'Horizontal mergers: Comment' *American Economic Review* **81** (4), pp. 1002-6.

Williamson, O.E., 1977, 'Economics as an Antitrust Defence Revisited', in: A. Jacquemin and H.W. de Jong (eds), *Welfare Aspects of Industrial Markets*, Leiden: Nijhoff, pp. 237-72.

Zalm, G. 1990, *Mythen, paradoxen en taboes in de economische politiek*, Public Lecture, Free University of Amsterdam.

Author Index

Printed and bound by CPI Group (UK) Ltd, Croydon, CR0 4YY

23/04/2025

14661006-0003